*Lonely Death
of an
Ojibway Boy*

ALSO BY
Robert MacBain

*Two Lives Crossing*
*Their Home and Native Land*

# *Lonely Death of an Ojibway Boy*

Robert MacBain

Robert MacBain Books
• 2023 •

Lonely Death of an Ojibway Boy
Robert MacBain
Robert MacBain Books 2023
2023 © Copyright 2023 Robert MacBain.

All rights reserved. This book contains material protected under International and Federal Copyright Laws and Treaties. Any unauthorized reprint or use of this material is prohibited.

No part of this book may be reproduced or transmitted in any form or by any means, electronic or mechanical, including photocopying, recording, or by any information and retrieval system without expressed permission from the author.

Book Designer David Moratto, interior and cover design.
Hon. Maria Minna, author photo.

Robert MacBain Books
www.RobertMacBainBooks.ca

Printed in the United States of America

Copyright registration: 1206236
September 12, 2023
ISBN: 978-0-9918017-7-0 (softcover)
ISBN: 978-0-9918017-8-7 (EPUB)

*In Memory*
*Charles Wenjack*
*1954–1966*

# Contents

1 Fatal decision, white students at residential school, Charlie's home community, children loved and cared for, the "stranger", Charlie turned loose, death from exposure by the railway tracks . . . . . . . . . . . . . . . . 1

2 Charlie's body identified, burial at Ogoki Post, restless student problem, students celebrate Christmas . . . . . . . 17

3 Students express thanks for how well they were treated, sign letters "Love". . . . . . . . . . . . . . . . . . . . . . . 23

4 The feeling of utter loneliness, staff felt called by God to serve at the school . . . . . . . . . . . . . . . . . . . . . . 35

5 Racism in Kenora, Indigenous people revolt, students better living at school. . . . . . . . . . . . . . . . . . . . . 39

6 Parents write expressing thanks for the way children cared for. . . . . . . . . . . . . . . . . . . . . . . . . . . . . 47

7 Former staff describe life at Cecilia Jeffrey Indian Residential School . . . . . . . . . . . . . . . . . . . . . . . 57

8 Positive letters students wrote around time Charlie Wenjack was there . . . . . . . . . . . . . . . . . . . 63

**9** Principal's daughter describes life at school, letters
Principal wrote . . . . . . . . . . . . . . . . . . . . . . . . . . . 75

**10** Letters from former students who wanted to keep
in touch with the Principal . . . . . . . . . . . . . . . . . . . 93

**11** Former staff disappointed after meeting with
TRC researcher, a Special Bible . . . . . . . . . . . . . . 101

**12** More positive letters from parents . . . . . . . . . . . . . 109

**13** Former principal defends school's record, respecting
Indigenous culture . . . . . . . . . . . . . . . . . . . . . . . . 125

**14** Final batch of letters from parents . . . . . . . . . . . . . 135

**15** Book in classrooms provides false account of Charlie
Wenjack's death, Trudeau government gives Gord
Downie & Chanie Wenjack Fund $5 million,
students think book is true account of Charlie's death . . 157

**16** Charlie's sisters support false account in Secret Path,
fabricated Heritage Minute on Charlie widely broadcast,
podcast attracts students from across Canada and in the
United States . . . . . . . . . . . . . . . . . . . . . . . . . . . . 173

**17** Schools across Canada endorse book, "Legacy Rooms"
featuring Gord Downie and Charlie Wenjack sprout
up across Canada, Mi'kmaq comedienne/broadcaster
questions Gord Downie getting Order of Canada . . . . . 185

**18** Book by Canadian author Tanya Talaga that is required
reading at some schools contains much about Charlie's
story that is not consistent with the facts . . . . . . . . . 199

**19** Author Joseph Boyden claims Charlie told him what to write and produces a false account of his short life and tragic death . . . . . . . . . . . . . . . . . . . . . . . . . . 205

**20** Three Ojibways from northwestern Ontario recount real horrors of their Indian residential school experience . . . . 213

***About the Author*** . . . . . . . . . . . . . . . . . . . . . . . 229

# *Lonely Death of an Ojibway Boy*

# Chapter 1

**ON THE SUNNY** afternoon of October 16, 1966, 12-year-old Charlie (aka "Chanie") Wenjack was enjoying himself on the swings in the playground at the back of Cecilia Jeffrey Indian Residential School in northwestern Ontario.

Seven days later, his lifeless body was found lying beside the railway tracks about 70 kilometres east of the Ontario/Manitoba border.

Today, Charlie Wenjack is the most famous Indian residential school student in Canadian history.

Books have been written about Charlie. Buildings have been named in his memory. He is featured in more than 50 "Legacy Spaces" across Canada sponsored by banks, major retailers, universities, performing arts centres and governments.

Thousands of Canadians from coast to coast "Walk for Wenjack" every October.

Children in more than 65,000 classrooms across Canada and in the United States are being taught about his altogether too short life and tragic death in a book called *Secret Path*.

School boards have incorporated lesson plans based on *Secret Path*.

However, most of what is written and said about Charlie Wenjack has no basis in fact.

Here, for the first time, is the true story of his short life and tragic death.

\* \* \*

There was no way of predicting how famous Charlie, the name his family always called him, was going to become back on that sunny afternoon of Sunday, October 16, 1966.

Two orphaned brothers were with him at the swings that afternoon, 13-year-old Ralph McDonald and his 11-year-old brother Jack.

Their parents had been run over by a train in the middle of the night two years previously. They were buried at the Ojibwa Presbyterian Cemetery at the opposite end of Round Lake from the Cecilia Jeffery Indian Residential School on the outskirts of Kenora.

According to the June 19, 1958, issue of the *Kenora Daily Miner and News*, the cemetery "is a last resting place for Christian Indians in this area."

Staff from Cecilia Jeffrey Indian Residential School took care of the cemetery until after the school was closed in 1976 and the property was transferred to the Grand Council Treaty #3. Since that time, the cemetery, where a significant number of Christian Ojibways were buried, has been neglected and is overgrown with weeds.

If you're not familiar with Kenora, it's an almost entirely white community of approximately 15,000 at the north end of the Lake of the Woods, about 50 kilometres east of the Ontario/Manitoba border.

The school, which was operated by the Women's Missionary Society of the Presbyterian Church in Canada, was on a former 60-hectare farm.

Most of the 150 students from far-away reserves without schools, including Charlie at the time of his death, were attending public schools in Kenora and boarded at Cecilia Jeffrey.

*\*\*\**

The Indian Act had been amended in 1951 to enable the federal government to arrange with the provincial governments and school boards to have Indigenous students educated in public schools. By 1960, the number of students attending public schools (9,479) was equal to the number in residential schools (9,471).

At Cecilia Jeffrey, however, a reverse form of integration had taken place. Starting in 1960, a significant number of white students were relocated to the Indian residential school.

In a letter to the editor published in the January 18, 1961, *Kenora Daily Miner and News*, Principal Stephen T. Robinson said a new school was to have been built on the Cecilia Jeffrey property to accommodate 50 to 60 Indigenous students—plus students from white schools in the immediate area to relieve overcrowding in the public system.

However, the project was delayed and, in consultation with the Jaffray Melick school board, it was decided that 80 white students would join the Indigenous students at Cecilia Jeffrey.

"Working and playing in these surroundings," Principal Robinson said, "have given both of these groups of children a good understanding of each other."

A local newspaper reporter interviewed two white and two Indigenous students in Grade 8 to get their reaction to the reverse integration process.

The article said the reporter had expected there would be both pros and cons on the issue "but except for some shyness on the part of the girls, there seems to have been no problem."

One white student said he'd been at the Rabbit Lake School until 1960 and was told he was being moved to Cecilia Jeffrey.

"I did not have any feeling against it," he said. "I am here [at Cecilia Jeffrey] and I like it. There is more to do, and we are able to take shop which I like. There are bigger playing fields. I don't care whether Indians or other boys are on the team.

"If I were asked to choose on my own whether or not to come to Cecilia Jeffrey, I would come."

An Indigenous student from Sandy Lake, more than 500 kilometres north of Kenora, had been at Cecilia Jeffrey for several years.

"I did not mind when I learned that Rabbit Lake [School] pupils were coming to C.J. school. I think it is nice having them here. If we go on to high school it will be good for us to get used to non-Indian friends before we get there. We learn more English with more English-speaking kids around."

Another white student from the Rabbit Lake School said she'd been at another public school before Rabbit Lake.

"I felt a little funny about coming here [to Cecilia Jeffrey] at first, but I like the girls and we all get along fine. One thing which I enjoy a lot at C.J. School is our nice home economics department."

A student from the Lac des Mille Lacs band at Upsula, about 350 kilometres east of Kenora, described her feelings when the white students first arrived at Cecilia Jeffrey.

"We girls felt shy when outsiders first came to our school, but now we are glad they are here. I have some non-Indian friends among my classmates. My sister has a very close friend who is a white girl. They phone each other every night. There doesn't seem to be much difference between us all."

By the time Charlie arrived at Cecilia Jeffrey, a new public school had been built nearby to accommodate local white students and Indigenous students who would board at Cecilia Jeffrey.

* * *

Ralph McDonald had run away three times since the start of school that fall. Jack played hooky on a regular basis. Charlie, on the other hand, had made no attempt to run away during the three years he'd been at the school. However, he did skip class at the public school he was attending one afternoon a week previously.

For that, Charlie was spanked by the new principal, Colin Wasacase, a Cree/Saulteaux from the Ochopowace Band east of Regina who had attended residential schools as a child and taught at two of them as an adult.

According to a report on the inquest into Charlie's death in the *Kenora Daily Miner and News*, it was a restless Ralph McDonald who took the initiative to leave that Sunday afternoon "because he wanted to visit his uncle whom he liked." The newspaper quoted Ralph saying he much preferred trapping with his uncle to being in school.

The newspaper also said that Charlie's best friend, 10-year-old Eddie Cameron, testified that Charlie was lonely and, when the McDonald brothers headed for their uncle's cabin, he decided to tag along with them.

According to an article that was published in *Maclean's* magazine in February, 1967, the decision to run away was made on the spur of the moment. "Right there on the playground the three boys decided to run away," Toronto writer Ian Adams wrote. "It was a sunny [Sunday] afternoon and they were wearing only light clothing. If they had planned it a little better they could have taken along their parkas and overshoes. That might have saved Charlie's life."

Three of Charlie's sisters, who were also at Cecilia Jeffrey, might very well have been on the playground that Sunday afternoon. If he had no intention of returning after the visit to the uncle's cabin, it is reasonable to speculate that he would have given his sisters a hug goodbye.

Ian Adams wrote that "slipping away was simple." It was.

During one of our many interviews in Kenora, former senior staffer Abe Loewen told me the doors were never locked. There was no gate at the open pillared entrance from the road and no fence on its north side. Nothing would have prevented Charlie or any other child from leaving the school whenever they felt like it.

In a letter Principal Colin Wasacase wrote to the Women's Missionary Society a month before Charlie's death, he said a large number of children had taken advantage of the warm weather "by staying away from school and wandering away from the premises." He said he hoped they would soon recover from the urge to wander "and settle into the school situation as the year progresses."

He wrote another letter a few days later saying the children had started to settle down a bit and only a few persisted in wandering away from the property whenever they pleased.

In response to his letter, a senior staff member of the Women's Missionary Society in Toronto wrote saying she recalled being at the school a few years previously and "it was very difficult to get the youngsters in for their meals.

"It was the kind of weather which must have made them think of home. I realize that it will be a very trying period for the staff and I do trust that while we do not hope for poor weather they will soon become accustomed to the routine of the new school year."

In a letter dated November 17, 1966, Mr. Wasacase wrote: "At present the children have settled down somewhat. We have a few hookey [sic] players but there are a few attempted runaways. We have been successful in getting them back all the same day."

Two months later, Mr. Wasacase wrote: "Things seem to have quieted down here at the school somewhat. There were a few who began to play hooky but have settled in after a talk with them. A few of the younger girls have tried a small escapade, but they have returned on their own. We hope the extreme cold will keep them in for us for the time being."

In a letter dated March 21, 1967, Mr. Wasacase wrote: "The students have not fully settled down as yet [after returning from the Christmas break] especially on the girls' side. A few of the girls have been wandering away from the school but with no real intent of running away home but only to visit friends or hang around town. These are a few who have started a few more [to wander off]. We are hoping that they will become settled."

Abe Loewen told me that Stephen Robinson, who was principal from 1958 until a few months before Charlie's death, used to arrange for sandwiches to be left in the bush so wandering children wouldn't go hungry.

He knew where they were and that they'd be home in time for supper. They'd most likely wandered away because they hadn't settled down after the freedom they had enjoyed spending summer vacation back on the reserves.

In fact, the senior boys had a trapline which extended all the way around Kenora.

Charlie and the McDonald brothers were free to come and go as they pleased, outside of classes, and this was, after all, a Sunday afternoon.

\* \* \*

According to the article in *Maclean's* and the report in the *Kenora Daily Miner and News*, Charlie and the McDonald brothers spent the first night away from the school about 30 kilometres north of Kenora at a cabin owned by a white man the brothers referred to as "Mr. Benson." He gave the exhausted boys something to eat and let them sleep on the floor.

They walked less than a kilometre the next morning to the cabin where the brothers' uncle, Charles Kelly, lived with his wife Clara and two teenage daughters.

Ian Adams wrote in the article in *Maclean's* that the uncle, like many Ojibways in the area, lived a hard life and, despite the modest income he derived from welfare and trapping, his family was often desperate for food.

He said it was obvious that Charles Kelly cared for his nephews and was uncertain about what to do about the fact that they were supposed to be in school.

"I told the boys," he quoted Mr. Kelly saying, "they would have to go back to school. They said if I sent them back they would run away again. I didn't know what to do. They won't stay at the school. I couldn't let them run around in the bush. So I let them stay. It was a terrible mistake."

Yes. It most certainly was.

\* \* \*

Charlie Wenjack was born on January 19, 1954, at the remote, fly-in, Ojibway community of Ogoki Post on the Albany River up near James Bay. His father was a fur trapper.

Ogoki Post is part of Marten Falls Indian Reserve No. 65. Starting around 1784, Marten Falls was a Hudson's Bay Company supply depot for traders from Hudson Bay heading to points farther south.

Marten Falls is one of the reserves included in Treaty No. 9 which covered 145,000 square kilometres inhabited by approximately 2,500 Ojibways and Crees. When the treaty was signed in 1905, the population of Marten Falls was approximately 150.

Here's how the treaty commissioners described the community in their report: "This is an important post of the Hudson's Bay

Company, in charge of Mr. Samuel Iserhoff. A number of Indians were awaiting the arrival of the commission. The first glance at the Indians served to convince that they were not equal in physical development to those at Osnaburg or Fort Hope [farther south], and the comparative poverty of their hunting grounds may account for this fact."

Despite the fact the people at Marten Falls did not fare as well as their counterparts farther south, a feast was held after the treaty was signed. Here's how the commissioners described it.

"At the feast Chief [William] Whitehead made an excellent speech, in which he described the benefits that would follow the treaty and his gratitude to the King and the government for extending a helping and protecting hand to the Indians."

Later in their report, the commissioners said: "The commodious Roman Catholic church situated on the high bank of the river overlooking the Hudson's Bay Company's buildings was the most conspicuous object at this post."

One of the four headmen who signed Treaty No. 9 with an X at Marten Falls on Tuesday, July 25, 1905, was listed as William Weenjack (sic). He could very well have been one of Charlie Wenjack's relatives.

In the 1930s and 1940s, when Charlie's father James and mother Agnes were growing up, people at Marten Falls lived in teepees and prospector tents. There was no electricity or plumbing. The only means of transportation was by dog teams, canoes and York boats.

Most babies were born in the bush with assistance from midwives. In winter, the newborns would be wrapped in blankets made of rabbit fur to keep them warm. Dried moss was used instead of diapers.

Homemade cradleboards were used to keep the babies safe on their mothers' backs. As they got older and started to walk, bigger cradleboards were made.

The girls learned at a young age how to make lacing for the snowshoes and moccasins and mittens.

The boys would be out in the bush with their fathers learning how to trap and hunt and cut wood.

The main food was moose meat, supplemented by rabbits and partridges.

In late September of each year, the families would head for their traplines and stay out in the bush until May or June. Game was getting scarce at that time. Families would sometimes have no pelts to trade at the Hudson's Bay Company store for food and other items.

The families would often get together for square dancing, playing cards, and renewing acquaintances. When the children returned home from residential school in June, a square dance was held to celebrate having them home for the summer months.

According to records kept by the Department of Indian Affairs, townsite planning and development didn't start until the 1970s. Up until the 1980s, there were no sewers or waterworks.

As of June, 2022, approximately 650 individuals were registered as status Indians at Marten Falls. Of those, about half were still living on the reserve and the others were living off-reserve.

\* \* \*

Charlie Wenjack was nine when he first attended Cecilia Jeffrey Indian Residential School in Kenora, which was about 600 kilometres away from the remote, fly-in, reserve where he was born. To get there, he had to spend about an hour on a plane and more than 10 hours on a train.

There is no record of anything Charlie said about the way he was treated during the three years he was at Cecilia Jeffrey. However, students who were at the school at, or around, the same time as Charlie wrote letters describing the school as a place where they felt loved and cared for.

A significant number of the students called Principal Stephen Robinson and his wife Agnes, who was the school matron, "Mom" and "Dad." Several signed their letters "Love." Many thanked them for being such good parents to them while they were living hundreds of kilometres away from their homes and family.

Parents who had attended the school wrote letters saying they had enjoyed their time there and appreciated the way their children were being cared for.

A teenage student at home for the holidays at a fly-in reserve about 520 kilometres northeast of Kenora wrote on the back of the envelope "R.T. [return to] one of your Indian daughters" and addressed Mrs. Robinson as "Dearest Mom."

Towards the end of her letter, she wrote:

> *Moms say hi to Pops for me and happy holidays to both of you. Thanks for everything you've done for me during the year.*
>
> *I better close off with May God be with You.*
>
> *Love.*

The letter was dated August 13, 1965, a little over a year before Charlie Wenjack's death. Her name, as with the names of the other students and parents from whose letters I will be quoting, is being withheld for privacy reasons.

Former students wrote saying they received letters from their children saying they enjoyed being at Cecilia Jeffrey and that they, the parents, had also enjoyed the years they'd spent at the school.

Students who had left to go to high school in North Bay wrote about how they were adapting to their new surroundings and expressing thanks for how well they had been cared for at Cecilia Jeffrey.

Former students who had left because they were needed at home, or for other reasons, like running away, wrote asking if the school would please take them back. Others said they wanted to come for a visit and renew acquaintances with the staff and friends they had made while they were at the school.

There isn't so much as a hint in the more than 300 letters that I have read about any child being emotionally, physically, or sexually abused by any member of the staff at Cecilia Jeffrey Indian Residential School.

However, as you will see later in this book, there was a significant amount of bullying. You will also note that younger children were reluctant to report bullying or any other abuse for fear of retribution.

\* \* \*

Charlie's best friend Eddie Cameron showed up at Charles Kelly's cabin Monday morning. He was another of Mr. Kelly's nephews and, according to Mr. Adams, this "gathering of relations subtly put Charlie Wenjack out in the cold."

Mr. Adams said that when he interviewed them after Charlie's death Mr. Kelly and his wife referred to Charlie as "the stranger." He also wrote that the Kellys "had no idea where Charlie's reserve was or how to get there."

As Charlie was with them for four days, there was more than enough time to get an approximate idea of where his home was by asking how he got to the school. He had made the approximately 600-kilometre trip seven times over the last three years.

If they had asked, Charlie would most likely have told them about having to take the plane and the train. It would have become abundantly clear that there was absolutely no way the 12-year-old boy could make it home on foot.

However, it would appear that no one bothered to ask Charlie how long it took to get from the school to his home.

According to the article in *Maclean's*: "Nobody told Charlie to go. Nobody told him to stay either. But as the days passed Charlie got the message."

I have often wondered why Charlie stayed with his friends and the Kellys for four days after leaving the school. It strikes me that he wasn't in any particular hurry to get home.

Perhaps, and it's only a perhaps, he might have tagged along with his friends if they had gone back to the school, just like he did when Ralph McDonald decided he wanted to visit his uncle.

In fact, if it had been raining that bright, sunny, afternoon of Sunday, October 16, 1966, he would most likely have been asleep in his bed in the dormitory that night instead of sleeping on the floor of a stranger's cabin. We'll never know.

On Thursday morning, Mr. Kelly decided to take his three nephews about five kilometres north to his trapline at Mud Lake. "It was too dangerous for five in the canoe," Mr. Adams quoted him saying, "so I told the stranger he would have to stay behind."

Charlie remained at the cabin and played by himself for a while, Mr. Adams wrote, and then he told Clara Kelly he was leaving. He asked for some matches so he could warm himself by a fire along the way.

It was late October and the temperature dropped significantly at night. All he had to protect himself from the bitter cold was a light cotton windbreaker. Mrs. Kelly gave him some wooden matches in a little glass jar and some fried potatoes mixed with strips of bacon.

*She's a mother. He's a 12-year-old Ojibway boy. Why didn't she give him a big hug and tell him he should stay with her until his friends got back from the trapline?*

Instead of striking east along the Canadian National Railways right-of-way toward his far-away home, Charlie walked north about five kilometres and got to the cabin at the trapline before his friends and their uncle arrived in the canoe.

Again, I take this as yet another example of him not being in any hurry to head for home. Or, for that matter, even contemplating heading east on the tracks in an effort to reach his family and home.

Mr. Adams said all they had to eat at the cabin that night was two potatoes Mr. Kelly cooked and divided among the four boys. He had nothing for himself to eat and drank some tea with them.

Let's bring Principal Colin Wasacase into the story.

During one of our several interviews in Kenora, he told me he became quite concerned when he discovered that Charlie was missing. He searched Rabbit Lake and other areas while an Indian Affairs official searched around the Rat Portage Indian reserve and the Keewatin area. Meanwhile, the police were trying to contact Charlie's parents at Ogoki Post.

On making inquiries, Mr. Wasacase learned that Charlie had been on the swings in the playground with the McDonald brothers. He told me he knew their uncle lived about 30 kilometres away. When there was still no word of the boy's whereabouts by Thursday, he decided to drive to the uncle's cabin on a hunch that Charlie might be there.

When he knocked on the cabin door three days before Charlie's lifeless body was found beside the railway tracks, he said, Clara Kelly told him neither the boys nor Charlie had been there. In fact, Charlie had been at her home since Monday morning and was alive and well with her husband and nephews at the trapline, less than five kilometres away.

Mr. Wasacase told me he still wasn't sure why she didn't tell him the truth. He thought it might have been because she didn't want to cause trouble for her three nephews. There's also the possibility she might have feared getting herself and her husband in trouble for not notifying the authorities like the inquest jury later said they should have.

According to the article in *Maclean's*, Charles Kelly told Charlie on Friday morning that he'd have to walk back to the main cabin because there wasn't enough room for him in the canoe. Charlie said that was okay because he'd decided to walk home to be with his father and wouldn't be going back to the cabin.

"I never said nothing to that," Mr. Adams quoted Mr. Kelly saying. "I showed him a good trail down to the [nearby] railroad tracks. I told him to ask the section men along the way for some food."

How could anyone turn a 12-year-old boy loose in bad weather with no food or water and without the foggiest idea of where he was going? Mr. Kelly wouldn't have put one of his nephews in harm's way like that.

Charlie was in one of the groups of boys that Abe Loewen was in charge of at Cecilia Jeffrey Indian Residential School.

While reflecting on Charles Kelly's decision to turn him loose on the railway tracks, he said: "He was the least likely to function in the bush."

\* \* \*

In the official form that he filled out to support issuing the warrant for holding an inquest into Charlie's death, Coroner Dr. R. Glenn Davidson wrote: "They stayed at the Kellys for a few days, and then Wenjack was told to leave. Wenjack was given some matches in a glass container and a map by Kelly's wife. It is believed he left about 3:00 p.m. October 19 [Wednesday.] to head east for Nakina, a distance of 375 miles east of Redditt."

One reason why Dr. Davidson had the wrong date—Mr. Kelly didn't show Charlie the way to the nearby railway tracks until Friday the 21st—was because the *Maclean's* article describing Charlie's trip to the trapline wasn't published until more than three months after his death. That important information wasn't available to Dr. Davidson at the time he issued the warrant for the inquest.

Dr. Davidson wrote in his report that one of the reasons he decided to hold the inquest was: "To ascertain if [Charles] Kelly turned the boy loose with no food to travel over 300 miles east, on the [railway] track."

That would have taken Charlie to the train station at Nakina from where he'd have to spend an hour on a plane to get to Ogoki Post. He had no food, water, or money.

The report in the *Kenora Daily Miner and News* said: "There [at Kelly's cabin] they were cared for and enjoyed trips to a trap line with the uncle. After a few days the Wenjack lad took his departure and started to walk along the single-track C.N.R. right of way."

Contrary to what he told Ian Adams, Charles Kelly testified at the inquest that Charlie had left without his knowledge.

Here's what the newspaper report about his testimony said: "When he took his departure, said Kelly, the boy was without food of any kind, **having left without his knowledge** [emphasis added]."

It's worth noting that Mr. Kelly's own diary said Charlie didn't leave until "Friday the 21$^{st}$." However, it appears that neither the coroner nor anyone on the jury caught the glaring contradiction in his testimony.

You might recall that Mr. Kelly told Ian Adams that he showed Charlie how to get down to the railway tracks on Friday morning and told him to ask section men along the way for some food.

When the six-hour hearing was over, the jury issued a handwritten report that said both "Mr. Benson" at whose cabin the boys stayed Sunday night and Mr. Kelly "should have notified the authorities of the boys [sic] presence."

They most certainly should have.

We can only speculate about what serious consequences there would have been for Charles Kelly if the coroner and the jury had known that Charlie had been at his trapline cabin Thursday night and that he turned him loose Friday morning with neither food nor water or the foggiest idea of where he was going.

*   *   *

Charles Kelly was the last person to see Charlie alive.

The boy only made it about 20 kilometres east on the railway tracks through snow squalls and freezing rain, wearing a light cotton windbreaker, before fainting and falling on his back.

The engineer of a westbound freight train spotted his lifeless body lying beside the railway tracks at a rock cut just before noon Sunday morning—seven days after he'd been playing on the swings with the McDonald brothers at Cecilia Jeffrey.

"Charlie must have fallen several times because bruises were found later on his shins, forehead and over his left eye," Ian Adams wrote in the *Maclean's* article. "And then at some point on Saturday night, Charlie fell backward in a faint and never got up again. That's the position they found him in."

Dr. Davidson listed the cause of Charlie's death as "exposure to cold and wet." He also said: "The deceased was not strong, and was very quiet and likely timid, as many young Indian children are who have little to do with town life."

Charlie was, indeed, a very slight, frail, little boy. It would appear from the autopsy report that he had contracted tuberculosis several years before his death. Dr. Peter D. Pan's report on the postmortem examination said he had a healed right thoracotomy scar where his chest had been opened. He had mild pulmonary congestion. There were focal pleural adhesions on his right lung.

Gravel was found on his face and mouth. His stomach was empty. He'd been dead for about twenty-four hours.

That was a truly tragic end for this young Ojibway boy who had no choice but to attend an Indian residential school 600 kilometres away from his home and family.

Especially when you reflect on the fact that he might very well have been alive today if one, or all, of the three adults he came in contact with after tagging along with the McDonald brothers on that bright Sunday afternoon of October 16, 1966, had acted in a responsible manner and notified the school or the police.

Charlie would have celebrated his 69th birthday on Saturday, January 19, 2023.

# Chapter 2

**PRINCIPAL COLIN WASACASE** wrote to the Women's Missionary Society on November 17, 1966, saying that they had identified Charlie's body at the hospital on the evening of the Sunday his body was found. Meanwhile, the police were trying to contact the parents.

Former principal Stephen T. Robinson and his wife Agnes were asked to come to Cecilia Jeffrey on Monday to tell Charlie's three sisters their brother was dead.

"We felt that both Mr. & Mrs. Robinson [who had been at the school from 1958 until just before Charlie's death] knew the children better than we and we felt maybe they would comfort them more easily than us," Mr. Wasacase wrote. "We at this time are still partial strangers to the children as we slowly get to know them better."

He'd only been the principal of Cecilia Jeffrey since the beginning of August. His wife Gloria was the matron.

Stephen Robinson contacted Charlie's older sister Daisy who was living at Red Lake, about 270 kilometres north of Kenora. A minister from Red Lake drove her to Ear Falls and the Robinsons met her there and drove her to Cecilia Jeffrey.

"In the meantime," Mr. Wasacase wrote, "an older sister Margaret contacted us from Sioux Lookout. We were also finally able to get in touch with the mother at Sioux Lookout hospital Monday night.

"The mother at this time advised that she wanted the body returned home. We took all the children to see the mother Tuesday Oct. 25/66 as she requested she would like to see them."

Sioux Lookout is about 230 kilometres northeast of Kenora and the drive there in the station wagon would have taken a little less than three hours.

Mr. Wasacase wrote that the police and Indian Affairs officials were having difficulty getting in touch with Charlie's father at Ogoki Post because radio telephone was the only means of communication.

Mr. Wasacase said: "We left for Nakina from Redditt at 6:30 P.M. [Tuesday] the three sisters and myself. The mother and two sisters Margaret and Daisy got on the train at Sioux Lookout for Nakina. We arrived in Nakina early Wednesday morning. We spent the remainder of the night in the hotel."

The ride on the train to Nakina with Charlie's coffin was quite an emotional experience for Colin Wasacase. It brought back vivid memories of an uncle who got lost in a blizzard and froze to death after running away from a residential school when Mr. Wasacase was quite young.

Charlie's mother and two older sisters had joined up with Mr. Wasacase and the other sisters when they arrived at the Nakina train station late at night.

They left for Ogoki Post on two chartered planes Wednesday morning accompanied by an Anglican minister from Nakina who had joined them to officiate at the funeral.

"The father was very upset as no messages had been received by him until the day of the arrival," Mr. Wasacase wrote. "I had also written him a letter Oct. 11/66 telling him that his family were all fine. It was after this time that Charles ran away. The father felt that I wasn't being honest with him and held me responsible for his son's death, due to my letter saying all was well."

When one of Charlie's uncles asked to see his body during the graveside ceremony, they noticed the stitches from the autopsy and concluded that someone must have stabbed him.

"So they were not going to allow the boy to be buried **or my return** [emphasis added] until somebody phoned the O.P.P. [Ontario Provincial Police] and confirmed what I had said about an autopsy," Mr. Wasacase wrote.

When the family got through to the O.P.P. on the radio phone, they were assured that Mr. Wasacase had told them the truth about Charlie's death.

After the funeral, Charlie's father said he wasn't going to allow sisters Evelyn, Annie or Lizzie to return to Cecilia Jeffrey. No one questioned his right to keep his daughters at home.

\* \* \*

According to the report in the *Kenora Daily Miner and News*, Principal Colin Wasacase told the jury run-away students were a major problem at the school.

He told of one occasion where 16 girls left in a group and, after they were apprehended, they made fun of him when he gave them a good talking to and told him he was being real "easy." That was one of the reasons, he said, why the strap was used for students who ran away from the school.

Mr. Wasacase testified that the children often found it difficult to adapt to the regimentation of school life after spending holidays back home on the reserves. When they ran away, he said, it was always a spur-of-the-moment decision with nothing planned.

A report prepared by the Department of Indian Affairs shortly after Charlie's death showed that 55 children had been away without permission on a total of 146 occasions in September and October of that year. The periods of absence ranged from a few hours to seven days.

Mr. Wasacase told the jury that Charlie and the McDonald brothers had warm clothing in their lockers they could have taken with them if they had planned on being away for an extended period of time.

In the letter Mr. Wasacase wrote to the Women's Missionary Society on November 17, 1966, he said that, in addition to Charlie and the McDonald brothers, nine girls ran away that sunny Sunday afternoon.

They were all reported to the police Sunday evening and all but two of the girls returned to the school.

"These two girls have both chosen to remain with their mothers," he wrote, "and continue school at home."

Mr. Wasacase told the jury most of the students, including Charlie, had been integrated into the public school system and boarded at Cecilia Jeffrey.

In a letter to the Women's Missionary Society dated November 23, 1966, Mr. Wasacase said Father Gaston Lebleu of Kenora's St. Mary's Indian Residential School testified at the inquest along with former Cecilia Jeffrey principal Stephen Robinson.

Father Lebleu told the coroner's jury that St. Mary's didn't have nearly as many runaways and attributed that to the fact that most of the students at Cecilia Jeffrey had been integrated into the public schools.

\* \* \*

If, instead of turning 12-year-old Charlie loose in bad weather with no food or water and no idea of where he was going, Charles Kelly had notified the authorities, Charlie might quite likely have joined the older children for an enjoyable outing to Winnipeg on Sunday, November 20, 1966.

In a letter that he wrote to the Women's Missionary Society, Principal Colin Wasacase said they took 60 of the older boys and girls to the morning church service at Winnipeg's Norwood Presbyterian Church and then they all went for a picnic lunch.

They toured downtown Winnipeg to see the Christmas lights and then went to see a religious film at a movie theatre. "They had a large area reserved for us," Mr. Wasacase wrote. "The master of ceremonies for the afternoon recognized us."

After the movie, Mr. Wasacase and the children attended a supper at St. John's Presbyterian Church, prepared for them by the Old Kildonian Presbyterian Church women's group. "It was a very lovely meal," he wrote. "Some of the children had never been to such an occasion and it certainly was an educational experience for them."

The group then took a walk down Winnipeg's Portage Avenue to have another look at the Christmas lights. When they got back to Cecilia Jeffrey, Mr. Wasacase said, they were "full, tired but happy."

Charlie would probably have enjoyed that outing with his classmates.

On December 23, 1966, 41 students who were unable to go home for Christmas because of the long distance and other reasons, were driven to Norwood Presbyterian Church in Winnipeg where they were met by Presbyterian families who were going to take them into their homes for Christmas.

"Rev. R. [Rex] Kreppe had appealed to the ministers of the Winnipeg churches who in turn announced it from their pulpits," Mr. Wasacase wrote on January 20, 1967. "The response was overwhelming as we didn't have the children to fill the homes that requested children for Christmas.

"Rex did a wonderful job in placing the children into homes with children of the same age. This appears to have given them a good lift as the children all had various experiences to share when they returned. We had some children who were having such a good time that they didn't want to return.

"The people had such a wonderful experience in sharing their homes at Christmas that they are wondering when they can do this again. We have had a few requests for some children at Easter.

"Some of the children have struck up some very good friendships with the children of the homes and their letter communication has been very good."

Charlie would also have been able to attend the Christmas dinner and concert Mr. Wasacase described in that same letter to the Women's Missionary Society.

"We had the concert with the various groups putting on their items," he wrote. "They had a visit from Santa Claus immediately after the concert."

Mr. Wasacase said the children had been asked to write to their parents inviting them to the concert. While most of them lived hundreds of kilometres away, some parents from the closer reserves came.

"The High School boys also put on an item which was nice to see as these were former students of the school," he wrote. "I am sure this helped the morale of the students present to see former students returning and wanting to share in our Christmas fun."

As you will see in the next chapter, it was not uncommon for former students to visit the school to renew acquaintances with students and staff with whom they had become friends.

# Chapter 3

**LET'S TAKE A** look at some of the more than 300 positive letters students, parents, and former students wrote between 1958 and the time of Charlie Wenjack's death in October, 1966.

Principal Stephen T. Robinson stored the, mostly handwritten, letters in neatly-marked white vinyl file folders which he kept amongst his personal possessions.

The last batch wasn't found until April, 2018.

I have read the originals of all of the letters and had them transcribed so I could include a significant number of them in this book.

The letters have been transcribed exactly as written, including typos, and grammatical errors. The names and addresses have been withheld on the advice of my lawyer for privacy reasons.

These letters are unfiltered, first-hand, contemporaneous, accounts of what life was like at Cecilia Jeffrey Indian Residential School at or around the three years that Charlie Wenjack was there.

I am sharing the letters with you, without comment, so that you can reach your own conclusion about what life was like for the students at the school.

We'll start with letters written by students.

\* \* \*

**Student** to Agnes Robinson: Back of envelope: "R.T. [return to] one of your Indian daughters."

Dearest Mom,

Just dropping in a few lines to say hello to you and to let you know I arrived home safe and sound.

Grandparents are quite happy to see me back, but I'm going to Mr. James soon again.

Well, I'll be only too happy to go over there. I like it there anyways. As for the news, while I was gone away to school there had been quite a few accidents here. There were two little children at the age of 2 and 4 who were burned to death during winter while their mother was out cutting wood and also their father was out trapping.

There was another boy who was a very close relative of ours who was drowned just late fall. I guess he was skating on the thin ice without his parents' notice on early sunday morning.

Moms, say hi to Pops for me and happy holidays to both of you. Thanks for everything you've done for me during the year.

I better close off with May God be with You

Love,

**Former student:**

Dear Mrs. Robinson,

I got Jemima's letter and I was surprise to see your writing. (of course) I still remember you.

How's Marie Lowell [Loewen] doing by now and your mother [Mrs. Robinson's widowed mother Agnes Ramsay lived with them at the school], I wish I could see her sometimes again. She was so kind and friendly to the children when I was still at Cecilia Jeffrey.

Everybody is fine here and as for my schoolwork I'm doing fine. We got our record cards last night and I'm doing pretty well! Only my writing sometimes is messy but other wise my trying my best. Do you still remember Madeline Meekis. She here this year. She used to go to C.J. too.

In Home Ec. We are making dresses, aprons and other things. I liked sewing better than cooking. I came the highest in Home Ec. in our class.

Every week we are allowed to make supper. I make suppers every Tuesday at Home Ec.

Goyce is fine here and he's always busy doing art. Drawing pictures and all that stuff.

The bell rang before I can finish writing.

I don't have much to say. So I'll come to a conclusion.

Write soon and say hi to Miss Love and Mr. Robinson that only if he still remembers me.

Your friend,

**Former student:**

Dear Sir:

My name is [withheld].
My age 17 years.
I finished Grade VII at your school.

I have been out of school for 1 year now. I wanted to go back but my step-father kept me to go trapping with him. He told me if you go back to school you never learn anything that will help you in life, but I told him if I go to school I know I would learn something useful. I keep thinking to worrying about not today but the next day and my future.

The nurse in charge of Lac Seul Nursing station and her husband they are my friend and they told me it would be the best thing for me to do is to write to you and tell you how I feel about schooling and see if you will try and make room for me this year. I worked for a man and he hasn't paid me yet so I still have to get this money to pay for my school clothes. I hope for this next week & hope for your letter. Please write the answer to Mr & Mrs P.T. Hay Lac Seul Nursing Station Via Hudson Ont. So I will be sure to receive word.

I would like to go to your school but if your can't take me would you try for me at some other school. If I don't go this year I am sunk. If I get my Grade IX then my teacher can help me decide if I should finish High school or to take a trade. I don't want the life of drinking and smoking. I want something better.

Yours Sincerely

**Former married students:**
(On Stephen and Agnes Robinson leaving after eight years.)

Dear Sir

Just a few lines from me and Marjorie.
As we are very sorry to see you go as you and Agnes been so good to us and also to everybody.
Another is we don't know how to express our thanks.
As you are the only people that really put us on the right track so here's hoping that we see a lot of you and Agnes.

Yours truly

**Former student:**

Dear Sir,

    Thought I'd write for I heard that there was a new principle at School. Here's to ask howes everybody over there. I'm just fine.
    Is it alright for me to go back to school, I know its already late but I sure would like to go back and start all over again as everybody's telling me I should go back and I believe they're right. And I realized that I need more education.
    I do believe that I haven't missed anything (in classes) for I almost completed in the seventh grade then I had to get out to start working at Hook's Camp. I thought that money meant more than school. But I was completely wrong at that. School means more. I have to stay at the seventh grade and complete it. It was almost the end of May when I had to get out.
    People tell me that I should go to another school and start all over again but I'd like to go back at Cecilia for I have more friends there and I would miss the school. I don't want to go to another school. But I'd to go to C.J. instead.
    I'll be back around this month whenever Fay Young takes the last trip to Kenora or takes a trip to Kenora. I'm working now and I asked the boss if I can go and she said sure when her mother gets here so she can take care of the baby. There's nobody around that can take of it now. Everybody's working—I mean girls.
    And oh yes my car coat's at school to. It's beige or tan something like that tan & black collar (corduroy cloth). And gold inside the jack or linen. It's my own jacket. So can you keep it for me please. I had rubbers of my own too but those are all right. I don't want them. Car Coat

colour beige or tan. More of tan. Gold inside. Tan & black corduroy cloth collar. Black round buttons.

I have to close now. Please reply as soon as possible so I can know.

God Bless and Keep you all.

Yours truly

**Former student:**

Dear Sir,

"Bonjour" monsieur. Well to get straight to the point or subject, the purpose of this brief note is to ask you about a sports jacket. I KNOW it was stupid to forget it but I was under the impression that I would get one here. PLEASE SEND IT as soon as possible; or do you think I should ask the Indian Affairs about one? I haven't been able to locate a Presbyterian church around here yet. Please send $25.00 because I will need it for fees, yearbook, school ring (unnecessary but desired!) a sweater to brighten up my wardrobe. Some of it for savings. Will be sure to spend wisely. PLEASE SEND SOON!!!.

Richard got ¾ of school supplies STOLEN already! [BAD NEWS]. He got into football team. [GOOD NEWS].

Good-bye and God bless you.

Yours truly,

**Former student:**

Hello Mr. Robinson,

    I thought I'd let you know that we enjoyed the trip down and we're adjusting ourselves to new surroundings here. North Bay is a very nice little city.
    Would you tell Mike to forward my check to the above address, please. And for my glasses do likewise for I need them very badly in some classes.
    I'm going to a very modern up-to-date high school. I reckon it was built about two years ago. It is strictly for students who are taking the general course. Geo, Willie, Ron are attending the Algonquin S.S. and I'm going to Chippawaw S.S. Geo & Bill live next door to me and they have to walk about 2 miles to school most mornings but I only have about ½ mile. Ron is closer to town and he has about 6 blocks to walk to go to school.
    About my pens, did you locate any of them? I'm using a temporary cheap pen until my other ones get here. All I actually need is the green Scripto. It cost $2 something and it is still a good pen.
    I think I'm going like this idea of boarding in a home because you don't have much to do in the line of tom-foolery so you have to read or study.
    I had intended to inquire about my brother going back to school to get his grade 8 at least. If he has written to you or maybe he is hesitate about it, would you write to him. His name is Victor [Withheld] and his address is c/o Ron's Freezer Service, Vermillion Bay, Ont. Tell him his possibilities of going back and standards required from him. I'm sure you'll do all you can. I'll write to him to inform him and to try to make him decide what he is going to do. If his return to school is impossible, you will notify him. Do that, please. Thanks.

How is everybody at the school? Are there any boys left? What happened to Angus Landon? Tell everybody we are having a ball. The woman, whew!! Something old for us old jokers (ha, ha)

Oh yeah, I forgot a greyish sweater on the line (clothes) when I left. I completely forgot about it. I wonder if you send that too if you can find it.

I'd like to say for the boys & for myself that we are saying thanks for giving us the helping hand while we were at C.J.

As ever,

**Former student:**

Dear Mr. Robinson,

I was wondering if I could borrow a pair of skates from the school this winter. I wear size eight and if possible a pair of gloves, shins and elbow pads. You see, I'm unable to get this equipment here on account of my not having enough finance. Hockey has already started here and I would like very much to play. If you cannot help me in this respect, can you speak to Mr. Law if he would help me.

The main reason for writing this letter is that I want you to locate my Bible someplace in the school. I must have misplaced it when I was packing and forgot to bring it with me. Besides the Bible, I forgot the magazine "Teachers Journal" or something like that line with some pictures tucked in between the pages. I would appreciate it if you could send my Bible anyway and if possible the magazine with the pictures.

That's all I would like to have. How is everybody at the school? As for the kids that came down to North Bay, they're all fine and doing well in school. Best Regards to all at the school

As ever,

**Former student:**

Dear Mr. Robinson:

Here I am again still wandering around with my hands in my pockets. Just got in Winnipeg a week ago and now I am trying to settle down in Winnipeg, till I get my papers all here and complete. Would you please, at your own convenience, go down to the Indian Office and ask for these birth certificate request forms for Ottawa? Not those treaty number proofs. Say hello to Darlene for me. As of yet, I want to join the air force and also the Manitoba Bell telephone System for a 5-year apprenticeship. Depends who will offer the best deal for a career and who asks first (ha).

**Runaway student:**

To: The Principal

How would you like it if I go back on January. And promised I won't ever run away again. Please.
It wasn't my fault it was that girl's fault and she showed us the way.
My principal told me if I can go to the school because I'll be sixteen yr. old next year. Because I won't be able to

go to school here when I'm sixteen and I still want to go to school and to Hi School.

I am sending those glasses. I took good care of them.

My clothes that are there 5 dresses 3 slips, 1 panty 3 pair anklets 4 blouses, 1 pair shoes. I red jacket, 1 tooth brush & toothpaste.

Please ask Brenda for my kerchief.

Thanks.

Answer

**Same student:**

Principal

I've been waiting for my clothes to arrive, even your answer.

I wonder if you could kindly have me back on January and promise I won't ever run away again and I'll be a good girl too, and I'll listen to the teacher, too. Please, answer right away before January and kindly send my things over.

Please let me go back and promise I won't run away for sure.

Yours thankfully

**Former student:**

Certainly was glad to get a card from you. I've been reading lots of books lately. Right now I finished three they are called "The Scarlet Slipper Mystery", "The Secret

At Shadow Ranch also, "The Secret In The Old Attic. Right now I'm reading "The Island Stallion." I only have four chapters to go and I have to wait till the lady comes again to collect the ones we have till Dec. 21st. They decorated the rooms already. I sure wish I was at school. Also I wish I could be in the choir too.

I certainly hope Miss Wier gets better soon. Glad to hear that Mrs. Steeles is back. Also that Mrs. Blake is supervising the junior girls. The Sonny Mountain Boys will be here between Dec. 28th and New Yea,r's Eve. I hope to see them when they're here. Are Mr. & Mrs. S. T. Robinson and Miss S. Ross back yet? Hope they enjoyed there trip [Illegible.] takeMary Crowe to Winnipeg? There isn't much happening here. So I'm closing you with best wishes.

May God Bless you and keep you.

**Former student:**

Well how was the trip to Montreal? [The girls' choir performed at the General Assembly of the Presbyterian Church in Canada in Montreal in May, 1964.] Gee I would like to know what did the girls do and where did you stay and hope you had a nice time yourself.

Oh yeah! I was very happy proud to hear the choir singing on radio on Easter Friday. I was singing away too, it was nice to hear the girls. Gee I wish I was in the choir too.

Gee it sure is nice to hear that Marie [Principal Robinson's daughter] is in engaged [to C.J. senior staffer Abe Loewen]. Sure would like to see her ring.

Well the weather here is very nice and the snow is going away ever day. We had a wet day last week and snowing to. Howz is it in Kenora.

My baby is fine. She's set up all by her self now.

On 14<sup>th</sup> I when down to see the doctor. I get trouble with my kidneys, but he said it not really bad yet. I had trouble passin water. I was in bed, so I when to see the doctor. I get to back some time in last week the month again. Guess I better go now.

Write again soon. Tell [withheld] to write.

With Love,


**Former student:**

I would like to know if the school still has the Bass Drums we used to have. I was one of the Band Members around 1936 and 1937.

I would like to know if there still around.

And would like to buy them.

The Band [community] here would like to get a hold of it.

To be used for ceremonial purposes.

I would like to hang on to our old traditions of having War Dances and Pow-wows.

Would appreciate ever so much of hearing from you, real soon.

I am yours truly,
Chief [withheld].

# Chapter 4

**WHILE TESTIFYING AT** the inquest into Charlie's death, one of the teachers at the public school he attended said he was a very lonely little boy and once told him he longed to return to his far-away home where he was happy with his family.

However, the teacher said, he seemed to change for the better after Eddie Cameron joined the class and they became best friends.

According to a briefing note prepared by officials in the Department of Indian Affairs, Charlie would have been allowed to return home if he had told the principal or a counsellor how lonely he was.

I found the note when I took another look at Trent University professor John S. Milloy's 1999 *A National Crime* which I had read years earlier as part of my research on the Indian residential schools.

In writing about Charlie, Professor Milloy—who was one of the chief researchers for the $50 million Royal Commission on Aboriginal Peoples—said department officials prepared the note for the Minister of Indian Affairs to use if he was questioned in the House of Commons about the February, 1967, article in *Maclean's* magazine about Charlie's death.

The briefing note said: "Had he [Charlie] confided in his Principal or the counsellor he could have been returned home. The residential schools are not detention institutions. They are operated for the welfare and education of Indian children."

The briefing note also said Cecilia Jeffrey Indian Residential School "served the Indian people with care and concern.... That

Charles Wenjack became lonely and ran away is not exceptional, for other children regardless of their origin, have the same feelings and reactions when separated from family and familiar surroundings."

Knowing that so many children had those same "feelings and reactions", why did the government think it was OK to ship them hundreds of kilometres away from their homes and loved ones?

Why couldn't they have gone to one-room schools close to home like the white kids in rural areas? Why house them in big multi-storey institutions?

In a letter dated December 19, 1966, Indian Affairs Assistant Deputy Minister R. F. Battle said that "the Department engaged the Canadian Welfare Council to make a thorough and detailed study of the residential school system with particular attention to the emotional and adjustment problems of the children, the matter of staffing and standards, and alternative methods of providing care for children who, for various reasons, have to be placed in residential schools."

Mr. Battle said the report was expected to be received in January, 1967. He also said it was department policy to provide day schools wherever possible.

"Generally speaking however, children admitted to residential schools come from broken homes, are orphans [like the two brothers Charlie ran away with] or are from remote areas where there are not enough children to justify the construction of a day school."

A former nurse who worked at Cecilia Jeffrey Indian Residential School four years before Charlie started there told me she felt pretty much the same way.

When I interviewed Gladys Ellis at her home in Campbell River, B.C. in May, 2018, she said: "I certainly know that it was hard on the children being taken away from their parents, especially the little ones. They wanted their mommy. They wanted their daddy. That hurts, and it hurt the parents to see their children being taken away and that was wrong but if I, as a Christian, hadn't been there to love those kids, who would have?"

You will recall one of the white students who attended Cecilia Jeffrey during the reverse integration project in the early 1960s saying:

"I am here [at Cecilia Jeffrey] and I like it. There is more to do, and we are able to take shop which I like."

It was Ms. Ellis's brother George McMillan who was in charge of manual training at the school at that time. He had an Industrial Arts Intermediate Certificate from the Ontario College of Education.

Back in 1953, as a 19-year-old member of St. John's Presbyterian Church in Toronto, Mr. McMillan was in the church choir and the Young Peoples group. That was when he was approached by the Women's Missionary Society to see if he would consider using his trade skills to help improve the lives of Indigenous children in Kenora.

"I know I made that decision on my own," he wrote in September, 2015, "however I also know that the decision was made with nothing but Christian Love in my heart and the desire to share that love and the knowledge that I had relating to carpentry and building construction with others."

After noting that it took two nights and a full day for the C.P.R. Dominion to make the journey from Toronto to Kenora, Mr. McMillan said he found himself in "a new world filled with people that I had never seen before and places that I could never have dreamed or imagined."

All of his family and friends were more than 1,800 kilometres away "silent and unavailable."

That included his father and mother, brother and sister, and high-school sweetheart to whom he later became engaged "only to have the distance and the lack of companionship sever that relationship."

Kenora was a truly strange place for 19-year-old George McMillan in 1953.

"A place where I experienced many lonely days and nights which brought on times of crying and waking up at night thinking it was all a dream, but it wasn't. It was for real. I was in a strange place with new Christian friends, doing a job that I felt led to and enjoyed."

If that's what being so far away from family and home was like for 19-year-old Mr. McMillan, one can only imagine what the experience must have been like for nine-year old Charlie Wenjack when he first arrived at Cecilia Jeffrey Indian Residential School not being able to speak or understand a word of English.

# Chapter 5

**AT THE TIME** Charlie Wenjack was attending Cecilia Jeffrey Indian Residential School, most white citizens treated the approximately 4,000 Ojibways living on the reserves surrounding Kenora in the same way whites in the segregationist states of the southern United States mistreated the Blacks.

Most restaurants in Kenora would not serve Ojibways. Restrictions were placed on them that were not placed on the whites. Seven out of 10 of the inmates at the local jail at any one time were Ojibway.

In an article that he wrote for the *Presbyterian Record* in November, 1994, Rev. James Marnoch said:

"In Kenora, the need was different. Native people did not live in town but visited it for business and pleasure. They were generally unwelcome. Hotel rooms and public facilities were often denied them. There was no place they could call their own. With the help of a board of people from other churches, Native leaders and community leaders, our church [First Presbyterian Church] developed the Kenora Fellowship Centre to meet this need.

"It would also provide opportunities for Native People to meet with townspeople to begin to understand one another. The church was present with the Native People in school, churches, on the radio, and in the town and cities."

Rev. Marnoch was minister of Kenora's First Presbyterian Church from 1958 until 1963.

Andy White, a former chief of the Whitefish Bay band, about 95 kilometres southeast of Kenora, remembers what it was like at that time.

"It was pretty rough," he told me during an interview in 1996. "There was a lot of racism. At that time, you couldn't go in the bars—most of us that were trying to make something out of ourselves, working people in real life."

Mr. White recalled going into an optician's store in Kenora and asking to have his glasses repaired. He was told that they couldn't fix them right away and he should come back a few days later. He then went outside and gave the glasses to a human rights worker who had been waiting outside.

"He was a white guy from Toronto. I would give him my same glasses and he would walk in and ask if they could be fixed. 'Sure, right away,' the guy said.

"I walked in and said 'how come you're fixing up these glasses and you weren't going to fix mine?' And then they would say 'well he had an appointment' or 'he asked me to come at this certain time.' 'But they're the same glasses I just gave you about two minutes ago.' They look surprised. 'Calm down', stuff like this.

"Same thing with the hotels. I walk into the hotel and say can I have a room? They say 'no'. Same [white] guy walks in there, 'can I have a room?' They said 'yeah'. So I go in and ask how come they wouldn't give me a room? 'Well, he had a reservation', they'd say. Bullshit. He <u>didn't</u> have a reservation. But that's how it was."

When I interviewed Fred Kelly, a former chief of the Sabaskong band and Grand Chief of the Grand Council of Treaty #3, in 1996, he described the situation in pretty much the same way.

"A lot of people were homeless," he told me. "There's no decent housing and there still isn't and where are they going to move? So, many lived along the shores, many lived along wherever they could to gain access such as they could and social services were not available to our people.

"What were we living on? I'll give you an example. I'm not going to name names here as to who I saw doing whom, but I can tell you that I myself was squatting in and around Kenora when I was 11 years old. I was living off the garbage, the best in the garbage that was left over. That's what was available."

As another example of what the Ojibway people were up against at that time, Mr. Kelly said: "For instance, you could go into the bus depot and you could see a bunch of people looking at the magazine rack. But, if you were Indian, you were told to leave. You couldn't do that. You weren't served properly at restaurants.

"There were certain places that you were made to feel you couldn't go and, in fact, there were places where you could not go. Things like, for instance, the beer parlours where we weren't allowed to drink after eight o'clock at night."

A point of information. Up until 1951, it was against the law in Canada for Indigenous people to have liquor in their own homes or to be served liquor at bars or restaurants. In fact, they weren't even allowed to enter a liquor store or any restaurant or bar where liquor was sold.

However, even when it was legal for them to drink, some bars imposed rules of their own.

Fred Kelly found that out when he went to a bar in Kenora one night and asked for a drink. The time was 8:10 p.m.

"I can't serve you," the bartender said.

"Why not?" Mr. Kelly asked.

"Because it's after eight o'clock."

Fred Kelly, wasn't the type of person to simply accept that sort of restriction without a challenge. He asked to see the manager.

"Why am I being cut off at eight o'clock when I haven't even had a drink? Why?" he asked the manager.

"We can't serve Indians after eight o'clock," the manager replied. "We find that they get too rowdy. They can't hold their drink."

"And I said 'so what's so magical about 8 o'clock?' So I'm an Indian and I can see it's 8 o'clock now because it's 8 o'clock, albeit Central Standard Time and not Eastern Standard Time [one hour ahead] which presumes that, according to Eastern Standard Time, those Indians in Toronto, Thunder Bay [on the northwest shore of Lake Superior], what not, would now be incapacitated by alcohol.'

"I was tired of being very sarcastic and tearing holes into this kind of theory. What is magical about 8 o'clock? Anyway, they apologized and they served me drinks and what not but I'm still not satisfied with that."

Mr. Kelly once went into a bar in Sioux Narrows, about 80 kilometres southeast of Kenora, with some friends on July 1st, Canada Day, and ordered a gin and tonic. His friends ordered beer.

The manager came over to his table and said: "How do you rate?"

Mr. Kelly asked: "What do you mean?"

And the manager said: "Look what you're having."

He didn't have to look because he knew that he was drinking gin and tonic. At that point, the manager took the drink away and told him he couldn't have it.

"Why not?" Mr. Kelly asked.

"We find our Indians behave better if they stick to beer," the manager replied.

A couple of years later, Mr. Kelly was on national television with Justice Minister Pierre Elliott Trudeau, who later went on to become Prime Minister of Canada, and he told the story about the gin and tonic.

"So everybody got alerted," Mr. Kelly recalled. "'Watch out for Fred Kelly because, if he comes into your establishment, he's here looking for trouble.'"

\* \* \*

In the summer of 1965, a year before Charlie Wenjack's death, the Ojibway people decided that they had suffered more than enough discrimination and abuse. Something, something dramatic, had to be done to draw attention to the conditions they were being forced to live under.

Some of the more militant leaders wanted to blow up the Trans-Canada Highway at Kenora. Others suggested dynamiting the railway tracks or one of the big dams Ontario Hydro had built across their rivers to generate electricity for people living in white communities.

The more peaceful among them suggested that it would be better to adopt non-violent means of attracting attention to their situation. They leaned toward holding a conference on the issues they were confronted with and a peaceful march through the streets of Kenora.

Everyone agreed that something had to be done to make the federal government in Ottawa and the provincial government in Toronto sit up and listen. They were tired of being treated as second-class citizens.

After considerable discussion among the Ojibway leadership, a consensus emerged that blowing up bridges or highways was not the best answer to drawing attention to their plight.

On a snowy November 12, 1965, hundreds of Ojibways marched down the main street of Kenora. The march was a terrific success and generated headlines in newspapers across Canada. Ojibway people were brought in by buses from all of the reserves in the Kenora area.

The headline in the *Winnipeg Tribune* said: "400 march for equality." The subhead said: "Kenora Indians air grievances."

Allan White, who would later become chief of the Whitefish Bay band, was convinced that the march—and the front-page headlines it generated across Canada—was a turning point in the history of the Ojibway people of the Kenora area.

"This had an impact on First Nations people," he told me in 1996. "They were successful in terms of that march. That was the turning point of the Anishinaabe [Ojibway] people.

"That was the turning point that the federal government and the provincial government finally opened their eyes in terms of political—not in terms of business and not in terms of the social fabric of life—but in terms of politics. That was the turning point.

"That was the awakening for Canada, for the world, that the Anishinaabe [Ojibway] people were the victims. Whether it's genocide or something like that, it's in the eyes of the individual people themselves as far as I'm concerned."

\* \* \*

You will recall when white students were relocated to Cecilia Jeffrey Indian Residential School in 1960 in something akin to reverse integration. Here's what Rev. James Marnoch wrote about that period in his article in the November, 1994, issue of the *Presbyterian Record.*

"Then came the government's integration program in which some local children began to attend Cecilia Jeffrey school and some C.J. residents went to local schools," he wrote. "The hope was that this cross-cultural experience would be enlightening and beneficial to both cultures.

"At the same time, students at Cecilia Jeffrey school who finished Grade 8 began to attend high school in Kenora. They were expected to board with families in town. There were such mixed results in this experiment, [Principal] Stephen Robinson sought and obtained approval for Grade 9 students to continue to live in the familiar setting of the residential school."

By "mixed results", Rev. Marnoch might very well have been referring to the racist attitude most whites in Kenora exhibited towards the Indigenous people.

In a memorandum he wrote on April 23, 1954, R. F. Davey, a senior official at the Indian Affairs Branch of the Department of Citizenship and Immigration, attributed the lack of progress in integrating Indigenous children into public schools in Kenora and other areas to the "historic factor that until comparatively recently and unfortunately still in some districts, the non-Indian community [would not be] prepared to accept the Indian children into their schools."

That is most likely why Principal Robinson felt that the Indigenous high school students would be better off living at Cecilia Jeffrey rather than boarding with white families in Kenora.

Rev. Marnoch went on to say: "The high school experience had a different effect on the boys than on the girls. Boys often dropped out of school. Trying to get home to the northern places, they would be stuck in Red Lake [270 kilometres north of Kenora] until they found some way to get a plane ride. If they decided to settle at home, they found they had the wrong kind of education.

"The girls, on the other hand, sometimes asked Robinson not to send them home for the holidays, but to help them find summer jobs. Some were afraid their fathers would arrange marriages for them; they wanted to stay at school. So the boys and girls who should naturally be in proximity to each other were being separated.

"It was becoming clear there would have to be day-schools on all reserves. The era of the residential schools was ending."

# Chapter 6

LET'S TAKE A look at some of the letters parents of students attending Cecilia Jeffrey Indian Residential School wrote at, or around, the time of Charlie Wenjack's death. Again, their names and addresses will be withheld for privacy reasons.

It should also be noted that, for a significant number of the parents, English was not their first language and many of them had only a few years of schooling.

The letters have been transcribed exactly as written and are being presented without any comment from me.

**Mother:**

> Dear Sir:
>
> I decided to drop a few lines so you know I'm still living, hope your okay too and I'm saying hello to Agnes, your wife and I'm a picture of me, see the different.
> This is my mother letter down here. I would like you to give my children some clothing because I don't have enough money to buy them clothes. That's why I'm asking you.
>
> From

**Father:**

Dear Sir, Principle,

 We are in need of help so bad that we are living in the Seul Indian Reservation which is now very hard to live in good condition.
 We are in need of covers and clothing for my kids and wife.
 I cannot make in any effort to make here either. The jobs are very scarce.
 Please send us a bundle soon as possible, cause the cold weather might come soon, on account of the kids.
 We will be expecting your great help at any time; during while we are—waiting patiently at the Lac Seul Indian Reservation. We were going back to Kenora and unable to make money to get back.
 I think we are caught in tight conditions.
 Well; we will be waiting patiently.
 Thank you.

Yours very truthfully

**Father:**

Dear Sir:

 Re John and Ronald (withheld) Band #292 White Dog Res.
 I had made arrangements with the Dept. of Indian Affairs on the 10th about my 2 boys. I won't be able to go in at the school personally on the 22nd when the school does close.

I talked to Len Robb of Pubic Gen store of Kenora. He comes to the reserve here at White Dog every Wednesday. He leaves Kenora at 12 noon and arrives at the Res. about 2 P.M. He agreed on bringing the boys in with him on the 23rd Wednesday.

Can you please arrange for them to be at the store before noon—Wednesday. Also I'd appreciate if you can send with 2 or 3 blankets.

Until I see you I wish you and all your staff a very Merry Christmas and Happy New Year. God Bless you all.

From

**Mother and Father:**

Dear Sir;

I'm telling you want I would like you to do. I would like my kids to bring some good clothes home because we haven't got any clothes for them here.

This was all I wanted to say to you.

Sincerely Yours

**Mother:**

Dear Principal,

We always saw your letter and answer this one. And I'm glad that you tell me about my children and others too. And take good care of the children how they from school. My children are always writing to me since they left us. And I never try to ask you some clothes that you give to the children on Christmas. Because I don't have money to ask you some for Christmas. Because it's kind of poor here to get money.

May God Bless You always.

Sincerely,

**Father:**

Dear teacher

I'm droping a few lines to you to let you know what I want you to do. I want you to sent my son is picture Billy [withheld] I sent him one dollar. That's fourteen dollars all together since he went to school. Please sent address and box number along with your letter.

Thanks.

**Father:**

Dear Sir:

I would like my little Caraboo to come home for a while as I am at home now & can look after him. Would it be possible for you to send him down to Glenorchy on July 30th I will be there to meet him. I supouse there would be somebody in Ft Frances to put him on the train to Glenorchy from the Bus.

Yours Truly

**Mother:**

Dear Sir,

    Just to let you know that Mary wrote only once since she left us here. We always write to her and she never answer our letters and we really wanted to know how she's doing. We also received one of your letters before Christmas.
    We want to give our thanks to you for taking care of our daughter. That is all for this.
    Please do take care of her because we sometimes worry about her and we also know that she is well take care of over there. Don't let her ran away or wonder around some place else.
    We are all fine and let Mary know about us.
    We are saying hello to you and May God bless you and all the children at the school.

                                    Sincerely yours,

**Mother:** (From sanatorium)

Dear Principal,

    Received your letter the other day and I was very happy to hear from you.
    I don't know when I'll be going home perhaps in a summer time and I am still doing fine.
    Everybody is so busy getting ready for Christmas.
    I am sending two dollars for the present for my kid.
    I must close now with the best of everything.

                                    Sincerely,

**Married sister:**

Dear sir,

Just to let you know that my parents received your letter and my sister's letter too, Victoria (withheld). But they couldn't read it. So I read it for them. We were very happy to see the letters. But my parents don't live here in Kas. They are out trapping. But they will be here at Christmas for sure.

I'm sending this $1.00 one dollar to my sister Victoria (withheld). You let me know if this money gets to you for sure. So I could tell my parents when they get here to send some spending money for their child. Not much to say right now. I must close. May God bless you all.

Yours truly

**Father:**

Dear sir,

I'm writing a short letter and I'm sending some money to Billy (withheld) $5.00 so he can buy something. I want you to let me know if this money gets to you.

I'll send him again sometime if I can get it some place. I saw your letter that you wrote to me in the fall
That's all I must close for now

From

**Father:**

Dear billy [withheld] Kenora School

    I drop a few lines to you too billy try to look after yourself and be a good boy. I don't want you to miss your school.
    Thats it.

Good bye

**Father:**

Dear Sir,

    We were wondering if you would let us have Elsie (withheld) and George (withheld) for the holidays. If they are interested. We will do the best we can with them.
    I am a towerman here at [withheld]
    The wife will be in Sioux Lookout June 27$^{th}$ to wait for them

                                        yours faithfully

**Father:**

Dear Sir,

    Try to put Anna (withheld) on Friday night's train. The wife will meet the train at Sioux Lookout Saturday morning June 27$^{th}$
    This is all,

                                        respectfully yours

**Father:**

Dear Sir;

    Please sent my kids back home, when they quite school for their Summer Holidays. Because next Winter I want them to stay home here and go to school here. The reason why I saide this is because both my wife & me, aren't well all the time, so they can wach for us when they aren't in school. They can go to Kenora School again when we think we will be alright.
    I will be thankful about it if they are all well.
    Please tell my kids Frank & Victoria we are still lisening. That is all for now.

yours very truly

**Temporary parents:**

Dear Mr Robinson:

    We are friends of Charles (withheld), one of your former students—and thought you might be interested in hearing how he has fared on his first venture away from home.
    He has been with us almost a year now—
    At times we know it was very difficult for him to be so far from home—but we believe there is a good possibility now that he will see it through until the end of the semester. We hope nothing will stand in the way of his finishing.
    He entered High School here in Lockport [Illinois] and because he was 18 and could not participate in

competitive football after his 19th birthday, he was allowed to play in his Freshman year—and won his letters.

He asked one day to be allowed to go to Joliet and watch a hockey game, carried his skates with him—and came home having played such a good game he was asked to represent the area on an All-Star team down at Springfield (our State Capital) where he played in a Tri-State League.

His own team came in second locally but he did much to bring it into that position—He went down as "an individual" on the All-Star team.

He is now going out for track—shotput and discus throwing.

He has been helping Mique build a shop—rebuilding machinery, etc., etc.

He attends church with us on Sunday morning and Sunday evenings & Wednesday evenings—most usually goes off with the Youth Group of another church close by—

I've told you of his outside activities and saved the best for the last.

He has just brought home his report card for the Third Quarter—He has a B in every subject (Above Average) and an A- in one (Superior).

What do you think of this?

We're proud of him too and we know his parents and brothers are too.

We just thought you'd like to know.

Sincerely,

P.S. He knows none of us ought to do anything <u>except</u> it be for the glory of God!

Another thing:
He has quit smoking!

We write all this lest <u>you</u> think at times "the struggle naught availeth"! Keep up the good work! And God bless you.

**Mother:**

Dear Sir,

    Just a short letter to you just to tell you Im very glad to hear my children are all fine I get letters from them They said they like there school I used to like it myself.
    I notice that cause they are good writers I had a letter from Edward he said he's in pee wee hockey team Im very glad about it you know what they do when they come home they are always writing so they could write good sometimes they ask me the hard word they don't know I try and help them
    Say could you do me a big favor could you kindly send me three used blankles I need them bad the reason why I'm asking you I don't have nobody to support us you could drop them at Health nurse's office at Indian office she's going to come over here at the Reserve on March 17th of this month
    I would appreciate it if you do that for us.
    That would be all.
    Bye Bye now

From

# Chapter 7

**WHEN I INTERVIEWED** former nurse Gladys Ellis in May, 2018, she said said she was raised in the Presbyterian Church and had walked with God for many years.

Like her brother George McMillan, she said she felt called by God to leave her home in Toronto and travel almost 2,000 kilometres northwest to Kenora to care for the children.

Ms. Ellis, who was 22 at the time, said she got on well with the children. "I enjoyed the children. I loved the children. They liked me. Girls wanted haircuts like mine. They came and asked me for boy cuts and it was just a wonderful year. I would've stayed if I hadn't got married.

"I helped a lot of kids there. Tucked a lot of sick ones into bed. Stayed up all night with some of them. Didn't get the day off the next day because I'd been up all night with them."

"We called [teacher] Margaret Love 'Love' because that's what she was. Fanny [Ross] was most kind to the kids, trying to make sure their clothes fitted and they were all mended and they were really nice people, good to the kids, caring. Agnes Robinson [wife of Principal Stephen Robinson] was good to the kids. My brother George [McMillan] loved the kids. He had a lot of fun with them."

In an article that was published in the February, 1984, issue of *The Presbyterian Record*, Ms. Ellis's predecessor, Kay Blake, wrote about her experiences as a nurse at Cecilia Jeffrey Indian Residential School between 1952 and 1958.

Here, for your consideration, are some excerpts from the article she wrote.

"Cecilia Jeffrey School was in the Mission Band study when I was a child. We packed a Christmas bale for the Indian children each year."

"When the inspector came the children were splendid, until they were dismissed. Then they all wanted to be monitors and swarmed around us showing sincere affection and shy respect."

"Our work will have a lasting influence. It was a difficult task, well done for the Lord."

"While relieving a grade teacher in late spring, I found that the children knew the answers before the questions were asked. There were not enough desks for the forty children. Orange crates were used for the extras."

"The children were familiar with me as their nurse (etc.) but some of them knew me from a visit on their reservation, (Shoal Lake), when I was with the principal's sister, Ellen Ross, who was studying Ojibway language, and I went to give the parents a chance to have me at their 'mercy', as we had their children.

"A dog used to get into our tent early in the morning and sniff us and jump on us. The children would roll under the flap and get the dog out without disturbing us....

"We were expected to lead in a service of worship in each home. Gerald Redsky was building his new house. When we arrived he stopped for worship. Later on that autumn on the way home in a storm he was drowned."

"Our choral speaking group were winners at the festival, trained by Doris Skene who also trained a choir that sang 'Fairest Lord Jesus' at my wedding. Stephen (not Steven) Robinson, (former principal at C.J., address in 1984, 1420 Ontario Street, Keewatin, Ontario), recently made a tape of these choirs."

"There were six groups of CGIT in the school. At a camp fire party we played 'Robin Hood' games using paper weapons. Our principal told us about his experience in India and showed souvenirs."

"The senior group was invited to Winnipeg. We arrived early—after a scout meeting or something. The janitor had not been told that we were coming. Our group pounced on the mess [food] and it was gone before anyone else arrived."

"The children enjoyed their chores and tried to do a good job. I asked one about cleaning methods. She told me that they wiped the painted wood with a 'dark clot.' I realized later that they were not hearing the word endings."

She recounted the success they had at Cecilia Jeffrey Indian Residential School in dealing with ear infections.

"I taught the health subjects and enjoyed spares on Fridays with the art class. Some of the children went on to become artists."

"Church services and Sunday school were the high point of the week. The children were naturally dramatic so pageants were special."

"At that bed time the Ibiams [a visiting couple from Nigeria] sat on the beds visiting the children. It was truly a love story."

"Across the lake on a grassy hillside near an old barn foundation called 'Bethlehem' was a favorite picnic spot. There were CGIT groups meeting with groups from town. A camp fire party with boughs of evergreen, with lighting from cellophane and bulb in a jar was effective."

Nurse Blake recalled recognizing the local Indian Agent when he came to the school for some paperwork.

"I realized that this was the man who took cases of Copenhagen snuff to the reserve to give out with the treaty money. I thought of the inflamed gums and stupidity of the students until we broke the snuff habit so that they could learn something in the classroom. I got mad and he got two jabs and an uppercut.

"He murmured 'You shouldn't have done that', and we got on with the second year requisition."

"Our wedding was during the spring break-up. This prevented a number of friends from some reservations from coming because the rivers were their roads, either by dog or canoe.

"We brought out a table where it could be seen to sign the register because it was not understood what went on in the vestry after the wedding. The little girls did a sun dance outside to keep the sun shining. It was a beautiful day and a happy one."

In February, 1992, *The Presbyterian Record* published a short piece by Ms. Blake who had had served at the Presbyterian Birtle Indian Residential School in Manitoba for 10 years before moving to Cecilia Jeffrey.

With regards to the school at Birtle, she said: "There were three Indian languages: Cree, Saulteaux and Sioux. We did not stop them from using their languages when needed. Visitors were always welcomed out of school time. Younger children were related to older ones in a buddy system....

"Some went to high school in town. We entertained children's groups from town and competed with other schools."

She also said: "We were a self-contained institution, run by a devoted staff of dedicated people who loved the children."

In writing about her eight years at Cecilia Jeffrey, Ms. Blake said: "A number of children had trachoma [A contagious bacterial eye infection.] which took several years to cure before antibiotics, and could recur. We were losing two children a year with tuberculosis; others went with it to the sanitorium for years. Two X-ray clinics were held each year. The government started eye clinics.

"There was an Indian health nurse from the agency who would help during epidemics as needed. Our doctor, Dr. Edwards, always came quickly when called. We ordered medical supplies three years in advance."

In another reference to Cecelia Jeffrey, Ms. Blake said: "A nasty chronic ear disease had plagued us for years. Dr. Ling, who held eye clinics at the Native schools, offered to help me with the ear problem.

"As a result, a five-year investigative and experimental project was started. We were so successful that ill children from as much 500 miles away came to be cured."

Ms. Blake got married in 1958 and left the employ of the Women's Missionary Society.

"Native schools had served a real purpose," she wrote in the article, "but now could be phased out."

\* \* \*

In an article that was published In the *Presbyterian Record* in November, 1994, Rev. James Marnoch wrote: "One day, during a junior camp which I was leading, an older Indian man stepped out of his canoe at lunch time. I invited him to join us. Afterwards, I welcomed him to the camp and invited him to speak to the children. He surprised me by saying: 'Welcome to our school! It is so good to hear the sound of children's voices here again.'

"He was James Redsky, a leader among his people, a former pupil and the father of former pupils. From him, and others, I became aware of the lingering fondness for the school and for our presence there."

Rev. Marnoch also made reference to his wife, Irene. "Irene spent three years at Cecilia Jeffrey school, one year as [girls'] supervisor and two years as teacher of Grade 1. She believed the Lord had led her there to be a Christian witness. She loved the children and still cherishes the rapport and confidence that developed with them. She was part of a dedicated group of church team players who, besides doing their own jobs, relieved one another on days off.

"Irene left Cecilia Jeffrey school when we were married in the summer of 1946."

# Chapter 8

**HERE, FOR YOUR** consideration, are a few more of the positive letters students wrote at, or before, the death of Charlie Wenjack.

**Former student:**

> I just thought of dropping you a few lines this evening, because this is my chance to write letters. We only got one more exam to write, and that is French, on Monday morning. "Boy", that sure will be a really tough one. I'm quite ashamed to tell you that I did fail my grade again. If only I had kept my mind in the first. Maybe, I would of did alot better.
>
> Since I came here [Teulon Girls Home] I've looked forward to come over on Christmas holidays for a visit, but its hopeless, because I don't have enough money to pay my way.
>
> Mrs. Nowels might think or she does that I'm getting along fine. In which she is very mistaken. It maybe not be nice to say that but I'm telling you the truth. My heart aches for "Good Old C.J. School." Instead of this place.
>
> I'm fine again. I had a bad cold for several days. Hope all of you characters are doing fine. I'm saying a big, fat, juicy "hello" to the children. May God bless you all.

**Former student:**

Dear Mr. Robinson.

I decided to drop a few lines to you and ask a few questions. I went to school in C. J. School and I moved away planning to go to another school but I made a big mistake in doing so.

I'd like to ask admittance back to C. J. School and go to High School in Kenora from there. I have talked things over with Miss Matthews and she says it could be arranged to make it possible for me to go back.

If you have looked at my record in the school, whether my behaviour has been good or bad in the past, I aim to make myself a responsible person and be an example to the up-coming pupils in C. J. I'll garantee you that I'm going to work hard and set a challenge for the rest of the student by going to school and probably to university. I'd appreciate it very much if you consider these things.

Yours truly

**Student:**

Dear Mr. Robinson,

I am really enjoying the summer here with the Hornings.

I was trying to get in touch with David [Withheld]. I am very glad to hear that Billy is back.

Would you please tell Marie [Principal Robinson's daughter] that Diane wants to hear from her. Tell her to drop me a few lines, too.

What about the High school pupils. Where will they go this school term.

I hope I come back a week before the school opens.

I suppose I will close now and I'll be staying here for awhile and if you want me to go to Chesley and I am willingly to go.

God Bless you all<br>Your Sincerely

P.S. Does the High School open on Oct 5$^{th}$? Do I go in grade 9? All these questions keep running through my head.

Thank you.

**Former student:**

Dear Mr. Robinson

I'm very sorry that I didn't write right away when I got here, hope you will forgive me. As you see, things around here are kind of tough on me, what I mean is the Grade 9 work and also being so far away from friends and the people I know around there, and sometimes when I come back from school, the only thing I think of is Kenora.

Well, there isn't much to say around here so I can't say much. Oh yes, if you see my mother, tell her I'm find and give her my address. Tell the staff I'm saying "Hello" to them all, and also to the Boss I was working for. Angus and George are doing fine as well and also the girls but, John left about two weeks ago. I think I didn't like seeing him go because that made me and George left, but when Angus got here, we felt a little better, but things are going back the same way as usual when we got here. So that's all I can say as far as I know.

Bye for now write soon.

from,

**Former student:**

Dear Mr. Robinson,

I do hope everything is going along fine there. I presume everyone is doing well at the school. As for myself, I am doing just fine and dandy.

North Bay is another Kenora on a bigger scale. I find it very interesting. I'm boarding with William Cromarty at Mrs. Roger Noe's house. These people are good to us and make us right at home. We live about a mile and a half from the centre of North Bay.

Regarding school work, I am 80% to the good. The rest is due to English and Chemistry, but I'll master them before the term is over.

The weather here is cold. It must be winter because there is also snow (four inches) on the ground.

Will you please give my regards to Mervyn if you see him. I owe him a letter but I can't afford another stamp. Also, give my regards to the members of the staff.

We go to Calvin's Presbyterian Church. Reverend Young is the minister. The Elders and the members are all kind-hearted people.

Will you please give me Mervyn's address. Thank you.

I believe I will sign off. God-bless the school and you.

Yours truly

P.S.

I'd like to hear from Miss F. Ross. Thank you.

In case I don't write for another period: Merry Christmas to you all!

**Former student:**

That was very kind of you for sending me a nice shirt and picture of the school for Christmas. Well I miss the old bell at mornings and the voice of Mr. Samington [Ron Symington] "Time to roll out boys, two minutes to get down for breakfast," If you are interested in what I did at Christmas Exams, my average is 57.4% with one failure which is Math, in the standings I came 8$^{th}$ out of 35. This time I didn't fail English. [Withheld] were here Sat. and he is doing fine for himself.

I heard that [withheld] failed five subjects, I don't believe it. I am doing fine, enjoy learning more of the way of living in a community. I realized that I owe you a lot for kindness and understanding last year. Forgive me of all the trouble that I caused you and the staff last year. And give my regards to all the staff.

**Former student:**

Dear sir,

I was quite glad when I received your letter. I hope you keep up the good work.

Andy wants a size-eight pair of skates and I, since William has a pair, would prefer size nine. I am wondering about my guitar. I have no use for it but to sell it, now. Mr. Noe has one here which I can play anytime.

Mr. Shaw called in at our place the other night. He says that we have the best reports yet. William and I are proud because there are quite a number of Indian people here in North Bay.

We go to Calvin's Presbyterian Church on Sundays. The people there are very nice.

I have to do my homework, so the best of luck.

Yours truly

P.S. (over)

If you see Mervyn, tell him he has a letter at the Indian Affairs Office. Thank you.

**Former student:**

I thought I'll drop you a few lines. Just a short note to you. Would you please tell me where is the Christmas parade. Just tell me the date and time okay. Well I'm doing fine here also the Wolfes family. I'm saying hello to Mrs. Robinson and Marie and all the staffs.

Well I hope youses are all doing fine too. I better close for now.

May God bless each one of you always.

**Former student:**

I am writing this letter to say hello to you.

Why I'm writing this letter is that I like to borrow those Indian costumes you have at school. I like to borrow them for two months and I'll take a good care of them so you don't have to worry about them we are going to the U.S.A. when we are done with them and I will return them you right away so if you lent them to us. Please give them to Miss Doreen Worden she comes up here once a week.

Thank you.
Yours truly, Councillor [withheld].

**Former student:**

> Now that I have more free time and I being all through with our spring term exams, I have all the time to renew correspondence with old acquaintances.
>
> I'm sorry for making such a long delay in making my thanking you for sending us the Xmas presents. I managed to play a couple of hockey games with the skates you sent but I had to hang them and used a pair from a friend of mine. During one of the practices I nearly killed myself because they were too soft in the boot. I had a good short hockey season. I started after Xmas.
>
> All the boys who you know from last winter are fine and doing well in school. Geo, Willie and Ronnie will be starting their exams in about a week.
>
> How are the boys at the school? How are the high school students doing at K.K.D.H.S. [Kenora Keewatin District High School]? (from C.J. School that is). Can you tell me where I can locate M. Ogemah?
> Well, I better close now and start on the other letters.
>
> As ever,

**Former student:**

Dear Mr. & Mrs. Robinson,

   Hello! I finally found out your address and had to ask everybody in the city. Ha. Well, I'm doing fine yet, and guess what? We had a four day holiday it's because of the teachers, they had to have their practicing of hair styling. We had a lady come to our class and she's a top hair stylist in the States.
   They have to work up to Sunday midnight. If I had known about this I would gone to Kenora. But anyway I'll be here next weekend for a visit.
   This is my fifth letter I'm writing to-night and I've been left all alone again. When I'm alone I lock the door and when the phone rings. It makes me jump.
   I've been doing Mrs. Smith's hair and she says a lot good complements from her friends in church. She really is a nice woman.
   You know she treats like a daughter and...

[Second page lost]

**Former student in sanatorium:**

Dear Mr. Robinson,

   How are you? Well for me I am doing fine. Sorry I couldn't write sooner but I wrote once and it came back, maybe it's because I didn't give the right address. I wrote a letter to Miss Yoder and I don't know if she got or not. Well I reckon I am to stay here for a long time well about a year anyways. One thing for sure I am taking school for correspondence courses in grade nine. In September I am going to have another X-ray. Every month we get three dollars to spend on anything. Well I am growing pretty fat that is in the past two months I have gained about twelve lbs. Oh, I made a mistake on the address and my address is [withheld]. that is if you want to drop me a line. Well nothing more to say and I reckon its time to say good bye.

Yours truly

**Former students:**

(Note at top of letter)

We good children. We miss you all. Love Maida. Answer right away please!

Dearest Mr. and Mrs. Robinson,

    Just to drop a few lines to tell you that I am very tried to write the children in school you may read it to them sometimes. Everybody is fine in school. We always love our teacher Miss Weibe.
    Today we wenting to a wedding at 11:00. Violet and Johnson Goodman. I don't know when Solly and Lydia are getting married. Maybe next month.
    It is very cold this month a little girl and boy frozen up they were found lying beside the path. Some of us frozen our fingers, toes and ears. We have to go two miles to get to school. Sometimes we don't want to go to school but we don't like to miss school.
    My father is very sick. He stayed in bed for two weeks. One week he never got up to look around and he never open his eyes too. Whenever he open his eyes he thinks everything is going around. He is very sick now. I hope you pray for him to get better. With lots of love!!!

**Former student:**

Dear Mr. Robinson,

As I go about my daily work here, I find it very inconvenient to be without my glasses. Although I have my old ones here, it would be absolutely useless to try wearing them. I would appreciate it very much if you could send them to me. There is not a very good chance of breaking them while I am here. The work is quite light and I'm sure I would be as careful as I could possibly get with the glasses.

Thank you again for the help I received from you and the rest of the staff. I really enjoyed the year I spent there and I look forward to next year. Thank you very much.

Yours truly,

**Former student:**

Mr. Robinson

I understand two of my nieces aren't very happy in school. I got a letter from them just yesterday that's Lorraine & Rosabelle.

Both the girls like school very much. They want to go to a different school Valleyview or Rabbit Lake.

I want you to give this matter your personal attention. I am very much strict with the school kids out here when they are in holidays.

As you may know I spent eight years at C.J. School myself too.

I had some rough teachers and some very nice.

There teacher is a little hard on them.

I don't want you to say anything to the teacher either. Just let it go by like nothing happened. But see to it they go to Valleyview or Rabbit Lake.

Teachers are like guides they can make a person happy. They can also make it miserable.

This I don't want to see. Let me hear from you about this matter.

We finally got moved yesterday to our winter quarters at Harrison Creek.

Everybody is well here.

Thanks.


**Former student:**

Dear Sir,

I take it that everything is going well. I have decided to write because I would like my guitar. Unless I am mistaken it is still there. I hope it is in good condition for I am sometimes invited to entertain some people. I know you are very busy but would you mind sending my guitar here. In case it is in bad shape, ask Daniel to fix it up
if he is still there.

How are the staff and the children. I am fine.

Yours truly

P.S.—I will pay back any costs that go to mend the guitar and to send it here.

# Chapter 9

MARIE LOEWEN, THE daughter of Principal Stephen T. Robinson, has many fond memories of the relationship her parents had with the children at Cecilia Jeffrey Indian Residential School.

"Dad used to walk around with a box of cookies he'd hand out when the kids were watching *Bonanza* on the television set every Saturday night," she told me during one of our many interviews at her home in Kenora. "They really liked Michael Landon playing Little Joe."

When she arrived at the school from Brantford, Ontario, in 1958, she said, the children became her family. And her parents saw the children the same way.

"Mom and Dad lived through their [student] kids," she said. "They loved those kids. A lot of the kids called them Mom and Dad."

Ms. Loewen said her mother was a very gentle woman. "Mom was the gentle heart." As her mother rubbed a child's hands and cheeks softly with lotion when their skin was dry, she'd say "Oh, sweetheart."

"It was like they were her kids," Ms. Loewen said. "She treated the kids like her own. Like me. They truly liked her. Kind of like she was their mother."

Ms. Loewen said her father could be quite stern at times and had a lot of responsibilities. "He would give me a swat on the butt if I needed it," she said with a smile. He gave her the strap once—but only once.

As an example of the heavy sense of responsibility her father felt toward the children, Ms. Loewen told me how he listened intently to the radio during the Bay of Pigs invasion of Cuba in April, 1961.

"What happens if we go to war?" he asked her. He was concerned about any negative effects Canada going to war could have on the children who had been entrusted to his care.

On March 19, 1965, the Catholic Indian residential school at McIntosh, about 90 kilometres east of Kenora, caught fire and burned to the ground. Ms. Loewen said her father sprang into action. He put bunks, blankets and clothes in place and took in 30 of the children.

"He organized all that overnight," she said rather proudly.

Contrary to popular opinion, the children were not punished for speaking Ojibway or Oji-Cree. Ms. Loewen said they were free to speak their native language in the dormitory, in the playroom and playground, and when they were out and about in the bush or in Kenora.

However, they were required to speak English in the classroom and when they were in the presence of a teacher or member of the staff.

"They were at C.J. with the intent of getting an education," she said, "The mandate was that we teach them English so they could function in white society."

When the students' parents came to visit, Ms. Loewen said, "they spoke to them in their own language."

She recalled a time when she was running the kitchen and the senior girls working with her were chattering away in Ojibway.

"English, please," she said in a friendly tone. They giggled and switched to English.

She recalled one shy little girl whose job it was to help do the dishes. Every now and then, when Ms. Loewen would bend down and whisper in her ear, the little girl would look down at the dishes and not say a word.

And then one day she caught Ms. Loewen by surprise by looking up with a little smile and saying: "Hi."

"When she said it, it was just magic," she told me. The little girl was starting to gain self-confidence.

The children were divided up in groups, with the older ones looking after the younger. The older one responsible for a group would get them lined up for different things like class and meals etc.

"Some of the kids were quite outgoing. Some were boisterous. And others were quite shy," Ms. Loewen recalls.

Because many of the children were not used to European cooking, she tried to introduce as much traditional Indigenous food as she could.

When some of the children asked her to make bannock—a sort of flatbread made with flour, baking powder, sugar, lard, water or milk—she found that children from different reserves were used to different kinds of bannock.

"Some kids liked raisins in their bannock," she said. "Others liked it fried and others baked."

You might recall former nurse Gladys Ellis saying that seamstress Fanny Ross "was most kind to the kids." Ms. Loewen remembers her well. "Aunt Fanny was my other mother." She also remembers Colin Wasacase's first wife Gloria "sitting with the kids on her knee."

We often hear about children in the Indian residential schools being reduced to numbers. "They only called me a number," former students complain in newspaper reports and on radio and TV.

Marie Loewen has, what I consider to be, a reasonable explanation for the use of numbers. First, she emphasizes, the children were always addressed by their first names.

That is certainly evident in the letters written by the students and former students. They never wrote about "#48", "#76", or "#123." They always referred to fellow students by their first names.

And, as you will note later from letters Principal Stephen T. Robinson wrote to the parents, he never referred to them by number.

However, when it came to dealing with 150 children at one time, Ms. Loewen said, using numbers for their clothes, lockers and other things was absolutely necessary.

The children were provided with a change of clothing every Wednesday and Saturday. "Underpants #22, along with shirt #22, trousers #22 etc. would go in locker #22," she told me.

Ms. Loewen told me her father had a very good relationship with the parents and kept in regular contact with them. It was, overall, a very friendly and informal exchange.

Parents would address him as "Dear Friend" or "Dear My Friend." One of them used "Dear Stephen." Another parent started her letter "Dear Robin, Robie."

Evidence of the positive relationship Ms. Loewen had with the students can be found in the number of times they asked about her in their letters and asked her to write to them.

In October, 1964, the senior girls organized a shower for her to celebrate her engagement to Abe Loewen.

"They gave me a beautiful salad bowl with their own money," Ms. Loewen recalls.

The affection they had for her is clearly evident in a photo I saw of her surrounded by smiling senior girls, including Charlie's oldest sister Daisy.

Ms. Loewen, who was a couple of years older than Daisy Wenjack, considered her to be one of her closest friends at Cecilia Jeffrey.

"She had a low, guttural, laugh," she told me during one of my trips to Kenora. "It was kind of funny. She was my friend."

\* \* \*

One day, many years after he retired as principal of Cecilia Jeffrey, Stephen T. Robinson picked his granddaughter up to drive her to school in Kenora. When she told him she hadn't had breakfast yet, he insisted that they stop on the way so she could get something to eat.

"He vividly remembered being hungry all the time as a kid [in Sussex, England] and said he would even heave from being hungry," Heather Bird told me, "so he wouldn't let anyone go hungry, if he could help it."

When some of the former students who had fallen on hard times met him on the street and asked for money, he'd send them to "Ted's" (Ted's Cafe, on the corner of 2nd Street and Matheson) for a meal. He had money on credit there for meals for his street friends.

"Many times, a drunk person would come up to [grandmother] Agnes's car window and she'd roll it down and they'd take her hand and say, 'Oh, Mrs. Robinson...' and give her a big smooch. I was horrified, but my grandfolks loved them."

Prior to leaving Brantford in 1958, Ms. Bird said, her grandfather was the manager of a community banquet hall and was responsible for staffing, purchasing food and budgeting.

"Apparently the [C.J.] school used to buy food at small corner stores in town, and the budget was insane. He ordered in bulk from Winnipeg and they were able to make a much better menu with way less cost."

Here is a letter Principal Robinson sent to the Kenora chapter of the Women's Missionary Society, most likely in 1959.

Dear Friends:

This school is situated on 150 acres of land surrounding Round Lake, within view of the C.P.R. [Canadian Pacific Railway] tracks where the Canadian and Dominion pass daily. We are three miles from Kenora, one of the most popular summer resorts in this part of Canada. Kenora has a population of 9,000 which is doubled with the influx of summer campers. Mr. Marnoch is the minister of our church in town and also the Chaplain at the school. Mr. Robson, a former principal, has a weekly broadcast over the local Radio Station, on which he conducts a S.S. [Sunday School] of the Air. Some 700 people are enrolled, and send in answers to the weekly lessons.

There are six preaching stations and at Shoal Lake we have an ordained minister, Rev. Stephen How, who is a native of Korea. We employ other workers on a part time basis—one of whom is an interpreter to the Ojibways. These activities are carried on under the supervision of the General Board of Missions. This school, however, is under the supervision of the W.M.S. [Women's Missionary

Society] and is therefore of special interest to you. Unlike our sister school in Birtle Manitoba, we do not operate a farm, although at one time we did and it was successfully operated. As you will notice above we still have the land, and will continue to keep it to **allow the children the freedom that is so natural to them** [emphasis added].

This school has an enrolment of 150 children with a staff of 24. Our academic training covers grades 1–8 and we have this year six boys attending the High School in Kenora. We have a program underway where 120 of our children will be attending the Township school. This will not happen however until September 1960 when the Township have built another school. We have an excellent Home Economics and Manual Training program, and are in every way well equipped to give the child who is slow academically a good basic training for life in the community.

You may read the story of Pre-Grade I in the November issue of the Glad Tidings, and you may show the picture of our Pee-wees who are on this month's Presbyterian calendar. That is our Senior Teacher, Mr. Hunter who is with them. We have a teaching staff of seven. We will need two new teachers this next September.

The student activities are those of any other school. Our children love hockey and we now have two registered teams and another senior group who play exhibition games. Our summer sports are limited because of the two months when the children are away. By the way did you read the advertisement in the February Glad Tidings?—look it up! Perhaps you have room for one of our children for a month or two. Jesus said, "Whatsoever ye do to one of the least of these." Send a line along to me for information. These children are from broken homes and the only home they have had is our "C.J." We need your prayers to enable us to ever be loving and kind with these little ones.

The Ojibway is a Northern Bush Indian who has not kept pace with the advanced industrial growth of the more populated areas. His living mainly is derived from hunting, trapping, fishing and logging, and therefore homes are at scattered points. You will understand this better when you see a shy little girl peeking around the corner and giggling. She hasn't met many people: at school she will; and this is a part of her training to meet people and do business with them. She also has to learn English, and express herself. For a long time she will say 'yes' for 'no' and visa versa. She will go into a corner and cry rather than see the nurse or tell the supervisor when she needs help.

On Sunday evenings we have Chapel Service at 8:30. This is for Intermediate and Seniors, and the people from town are invited out to sing hymns and afterwards to stay and have a cup of tea with six boys and six girls who are chosen to serve and mingle with them. It's too bad that your group could not drop in some Sunday evening and enjoy this old-fashioned fellowship. You would meet Miss Ross our Deaconess who has served faithfully at the school for some 9 years; her sister Miss Fanny Ross who works in the sewing room with Miss Chambers; the Supervisors of our Senior children (the other two supervisors are putting the Juniors to bed, leading them in prayers and getting them settled); Miss Simpson would be in her usual place at the piano; and our Miss Love would be working in the background. Others of the staff are not there because of their various duties at home or in their Church life. Among those are Miss Skene, Mr. Hunter, Mr. & Mrs. [George] McMillan and our nurse Miss [Gladys] McMillan.

In this brief letter you have visited our school or should I say "Your school" yours particularly; for you are a tax payer and therefore your tax dollar helps finance it and yours a second time for your Auxiliary is one of many who form a group who have the God-given responsibility of administering it. And then again our problems are also yours and we therefore need your fellowship in prayer.

As we pray let us:
- Pray that God will purify us and make us clean channels through which he can move and do His will.
- Ask Him to send us His "Called ones"—people who will love these children and give of themselves to assist us in forming a team to administer in your name.
- Remember your group and all groups who form the whole unit of the W.M.S.; also our own Church as it ministers ever in broader spheres of service.
- Thank Him for past mercies: for providing this field of service: for interested friends: for faith and vision to look into the future knowing that He will be more than we can ask or think.

The foregoing is sent with greetings from the staff and children of C. J. School.

Stephen T. Robinson,<br>Principal.

STR/hr


Here is a letter Principal Robinson sent to all of the parents on January 22, 1962.

To Parent or Guardian.
Dear Parent or Guardian:

You will be interested in knowing that most of the children have been good and have done fairly well in their school work. You will find the school report enclosed. Those who have low marks will be given extra work so that the next report should be more favourable.

All the children who were not able to go home at Christmas were invited at some time during the holidays to the homes of white people in our community. I am sure you will be happy to know that they are very fond of your children and many have been invited back to the homes for either a weekend or for the Easter holidays.

Most of the children have been quite healthy and I am sure you will be surprised at how much they have grown.

Although your child is quite healthy now, in the event of the need of Medical or Dental treatment I have no authority to grant this permission. If you agree to grant me this authority will you kindly sign the enclosed form and return it in the enclosed envelope. I would enjoy receiving a letter from you also.

You can be assured that we all love your children and do our best to help them to become good useful citizens who are **proud of their Indian heritage** [emphasis added].

Yours very truly,

Stephen T. Robinson,
Principal.

Encl.
STR/hr

**NOTE:** On Tuesday, April 11, 2023, I spent two hours at the Toronto archives of the Presbyterian Church in Canada. There were quite a few photos showing Cecilia Jeffrey students celebrating their culture in authentic Indigenous regalia.

A few of the photos showed students wearing full-feathered headdresses on a float the school entered in a parade in Kenora.

Seeing the photos reminded me of the band councillor who wrote asking if he could borrow some of the costumes to use on the powwow circuit in the United States.

I also saw a significant number of unposed photos of happy, smiling, well-fed, well-clothed children at Cecilia Jeffrey Indian Residential School.

The photos bore witness to the way the school was described in the more than 300 letters from students and parents during the eight years Stephen T. Robinson was the principal of Cecilia Jeffrey Indian Residential school.

They also demonstrate the fulfillment of Principal Robinson's pledge to the parents that the staff at Cecilia Jeffrey would "love your children and do our best to help them to become good useful citizens who are proud of their Indian heritage."

Here are a few more of the letters Principal Robinson wrote during the eight years that he was at the school.

Dear [withheld]

After the busy Christmas season I am writing to let you know that Shirley is in good health, and very happy.

We are sorry that she got so many of the children's diseases, but that is quite usual in a school where we have so many children together.

We bought her a lovely doll for Christmas and put the remainder of the money in her bank here. She now has $13.00. With this she is able to buy candy each week at the tuck shop.

Miss Weir, one of our supervisors, will take a picture of Shirley and we will send it along to you.

I hope you are having a good winter and please give my regards to Mrs. [withheld].

Best wishes for the New Year.

Yours truly,
Stephen T. Robinson,
Principal

Dear Mr. [withheld]:

I am writing you in answer to your question about Mary's weight. I have checked with our nurse and since last fall when she arrived at school, she has grown 1 ½ inches and has gained 5 pounds in weight.

She, no doubt, would appear to be thinner because she has grown taller. Her health and behaviour are both good and you need not worry about her while she is here. Most of the children here get more food and are warmer here than in their own homes.

We appreciate the interest you have taken in Mary and you can rest assured that she will return to you in June a healthy and bright girl. We also treasure your thought and prayer for us and the children.

Sincerely yours,<br>
Stephen T. Robinson<br>
Principal

STR/hr


Dear Mr. [withheld]:

Madeline has been well but she did foolishly run away with two other girls and stayed out all night without her pills.

She is now studying hard for her exams and they will both be home on June 30$^{th}$. I hope you have a pleasant summer with them.

Lydia is a very lovely little girl.

Yours truly,<br>
Stephen T. Robinson<br>
Principal.

Dear Mr. [withheld]

I must apologize for not writing before but we have been so busy at the school with one of our Staff in the hospital.

Penny came home from the hospital on Friday and she is perfectly alright now. She had an infection in her ankle and it took some time to clear up.

She is quite happy here and there is no reason for any concern for her. I will try and get a picture taken so that I can send it to you.

Yours very truly,
Stephen T. Robinson,
Principal.

STR/hr


STR/hr


Dear Mr. [withheld]

Your daughter Victoria will be spending the summer with your son Allen in Unaka. Jeannie will be working here in Kenora but will be in Ft. William for three days in August. She will come to see you then.

Jeannie has a position as a housekeeper for a lady in Kenora. We will watch her and when she comes out to the school to visit us we will encourage her to write to you.

They are both well.

Yours truly,
Stephen T. Robinson
Principal.

STR/hr

Dear [withheld]:

I did receive your telegram at Christmas time with many other requests for children to be home for the holiday season. Money is not provided for travelling except for coming to school in September and returning in June. Therefore they could not come.

We had eighty children in the school for Christmas and they all had a good time.

Your children are doing well in school and you will be pleased to know that they are in good health.

I hope this answers your question.

Yours truly,<br>
Stephen T. Robinson<br>
Principal.

STR/hr


Dear [withheld]:

Your son George [withheld] left by bus this morning to return home. He said he was needed there for two or three weeks and would return after the work had been completed.

He was granted permission to go on his own word that he was needed there. I must however have a letter from you confirming this and with the promise that he will return as soon as possible, otherwise I must report him as a truant.

He is doing very well in his school work and you and I know that he needs all he can get to prepare him for a better life.

Please write me as soon as possible.

Yours truly,<br>
Stephen T. Robinson,<br>
Principal.

Dear [withheld]:

I would like to know the reason why Maida was not returned to school in January. We have given you a full month to have her here.

We operate the school on a full year basis and expect our students to attend for the whole year. I must inform you that if she does not return we cannot guarantee a place for her in September. We have quite a number of children waiting to come in and stay for the full term.

Please reply stating the reason for her truancy and your intention for her in the future.

Yours truly,
Stephen T. Robinson,
Principal.


Dear [withheld]

I was sorry to hear that Albert got into trouble and also the other boys.

With regard to Margaret and Mary—We want them to stay until the closing of school. They have been very good girls, and you should be particularly proud, of Margaret. She has developed into a very sensible girl and she wants to stay and complete Grade 4.

It is very important that the children get their grades, and I know that you as a good father to these children will be patient for the few weeks remaining.

Yours truly,
Stephen T. Robinson,
Principal.

Dear [withheld]

I was sorry that you left this school so quickly. I was also surprised because when you came that first day I thought you would be the kind of girl who would stay and be a good student.

It is impossible for you to return now, and I will return your clothing as soon as you return Lilas [withheld] glasses.

I hope you are going to school now.

Yours truly,<br>
Stephen T. Robinson,<br>
Principal.

Dear [withheld]

Your daughter Rosella is absent from school without permission. Her attitude so far has been good, and she is taking Grade 7 work which requires all the effort and time she can devote to study and attendance in class.

If she continues with this truancy, I must recommend that she be discharged from the school. She not only deprives herself of an education but also another child who could be here in her place.

She left about 9:30 on Saturday evening with Julia Greene.

Yours very truly,<br>
Stephen T. Robinson,<br>
Principal.

Dear [withheld]:

Your daughter Julia is absent from school without permission. She has already lost three days of schooling when she was not returned after the Thanksgiving holiday.

I would impress on you the importance of her regular attendance at school especially if she intends to continue through High School.

She and Rosella [withheld] left the school about 9:30 on Saturday evening after we had a party for their supervisor.

Yours very truly,
Stephen T. Robinson,
Principal.

Dear [withheld]:

It is now about two weeks since your son Douglas left the school with two other boys. The others have been returned and I request that your boy be returned immediately.

You are well aware of the care your children received here and I would hope that you will cooperate in having this boy returned to attend school on Monday, November 4$^{th}$.

It would also be appreciated if you would impress on this boy the danger of wandering away from the school without permission.

Yours very truly,
Stephen T. Robinson,
Principal.

Dear [withheld]:

Rosella has been absent from the school since Saturday October 19th.

If she is not returned to attend class on Monday Nov. 4th I must ask that she be discharged from this school.

I know she has not returned home, but this letter is to inform you of her absence from school and to warn you of the action we must take.

This is the third year that Rosella has failed to cooperate with those who wish to assist her in receiving a reasonable standard of education.

If you know of her whereabouts will you kindly communicate with me.

> Yours very truly,
> Stephen T. Robinson,
> Principal.

Dear [withheld]:

I was pleased to get your letter and thank you on behalf of the staff for the kind words your said about them. It is very good to know that in after years our students do realize what has been done for them.

Lorraine was talking about you yesterday, and telling us of your adopted children. We wish you and your family every success.

To answer your questions with regard to the school:

1. The school is now financed by the Department of Indian Affairs. In 1958 they changed the system of operation and now a budget is set up for each school and the Principal endeavours to operate within that budget. Some items of interest would be:

(a) Food allowance, child under 13—42 ¢ per day
                          13 and over—53 ¢ per day
   (b) Clothing, child under 13—$13.39 per quarter
                          13 and over—$19.69 per quarter
   (c) Allowance for extra curricular activities—approximately $10.00 per student per year; this includes purchase of T.V. sets, radios, records, hockey equipment, etc.

2. The Indian Affairs Branch will assist the Treaty Indian student on into University if he is capable and conscientious. As you may know our children are integrated into the Township school system and attend white schools at Grade 2 level. We now have only one teacher (Grade 1) but we have a Teacher Counsellor who assists these pupils in their home study and tutors them in difficult subjects, and also gives them some guidance.

# Chapter 10

**HERE ARE A** few more letters from former students of Cecilia Jeffrey Indian Residential School.

It is clear that they wanted to keep in touch with Principal Robinson and fully expected that he would be interested in knowing how they were doing.

**Former student:**

> Dear Sir:
>
> I finally got around to writing and managed to scrape up a five dollar bill. I'm enclosing a five dollar money order for the cleaning and shipment of my winter jacket, which I left at the school.
>
> Yours truly,

P.S. Getting along well.

**Former student:**

Dear Sir,

I'm writing to inform you where I'm staying. I had a fairly enjoyable trip down [to North Bay] and it didn't take long to settle down. I think the people I'm staying with are very nice. There are three kids in the house most of the time. I don't think they'll bother me too much. The older boy seems to know how to look after his younger brother and sister.

About my coat, I forgot to leave the money to Mrs Robinson to give to you. When I got to North Bay I found out I had to buy my own clothes. So I had to buy some clothes to hold me till my next pay-check. At that time, I will be able to send the money.

Well, that about winds up what I have to say.

My regards to everyone at the school.

Yours truly,

**Former student:**

Dear Mr & Mrs Robinson,

I think it's a wonderful thing to have someone to write to especially when you have so many problems. First, I want to find out how the staff are doing over there. I guess you two and Marie [Principal Robinson's daughter.] are the only people at the school.

Rosie and I haven't been enjoying our holidays too much. I've been so upset for the past few weeks on account of all the drunkenness going on down here. I'm telling you it's so terrible.

Margaret and I were home alone for about five days keeping Rosie & my little brother and my married sister's children. Gladys was in jail at International Falls for a few days because of quarrelling with her husband. Her little baby was sick while she was away so Marge and I had to walk to Emo along with the little boy. He was taken in to the hospital right away. The others weren't quite well either. So that made things worse.

In that time my parents were at Fort Frances on a drunken spree. I can't stop them. I try to talk to my dad sometimes but he gets angry always telling me not to tell him what to do. Someday I'm going to leave them for good. I sure wish I could go back and finish my grade eight. Same with Margaret she was very disappointed about quitting school.

I wonder if you could give Margaret a job over there. She hates to stay with her parents any more. She'd be better off if she was working someplace. She got permission from her parents already. She will be sixteen this year.

I think Margaret and I will be looking for a cheap job anyway that is if you do not want to hire her or want me back at school. I don't blame you and Mrs Robinson for not wishing me back to school in Sept. I have done so much to hurt you people. I have realized how much I must've hurt you all and I'm terribly sorry. I don't think I deserve your forgiveness. I think it would be the most precious gift from you people.

I received the certificate and the eight dollars this year. I guess that was the Doner Prize. I used the money for some groceries anyway.

I do hope you reply soon. God bless.

Sincerely,

Send the letter to
Nestor Falls, Ont
c/o Black Bear Camp

We're moving over there.
My dad has sobered up for a while anyway.

**Former student in reformatory:**

Dear Sir,

Thought I'd drop a few lines to you. I think you are the one that could help me on my problem. I wonder if you would give me employment in the near future.

I would like a job when I am released from here. I don't want to back to where I been work. I'll only be getting into trouble again.

I only don't want to back there, because don't want to be anywhere where there are drinking people. I want to quit drinking. I think I can do it. Nobody can make me quit drinking. If I want to quit drink, not only me. That includes on everybody that drinks. Like I know through experience of drink. I will have to make myself to quit.

You probably know by now that I made an inquiry in taking some kind of "course" when I am release from the reformatory. That is if I am lucky enough.

The reason why I am saying is I would like to be where are books for me to read. Just in case they put me through in taking the course in carpentry.

So now, please answer. My date of release falls on July 28. I best close for now.

Please write when have received this letter.

I remain as ever.

Your truly


**Former student:**

Dear Sir,

I thought of asking you if you could find me a job in Kenora. My parents said it would be alright if you found one for me. But I wouldn't want a job at the school. So, would you please try and do the best you can? I'd rather work than go to school as I didn't do very well in my exams.

Yours truly,

P.S. Please write soon &
let me know.

**Former student:**

Dear Sir,

We all came back safely. Thank you for keeping and guiding us. I wonder if I had some money left. Henry had $2.55 and I had $2.10. But I didn't have mine. Henry has his. Good-bye.

Yours truly

**Former student:**

Dear Principal;

Just a few lines to you this evening I wonder if you'd be interested to help me. You see I'm taking a correspondence course from Toronto. You see I just had my grade VII completely finished at C. J. School so I wonder if you'd sent me my report card. Maybe if you look up the old forms. I left school in 1952 and I would like to ask you grade VIII books and I'll return them back when I'm through grade VIII work. Maybe perhaps you'd sent with Mary Crowe and I'll go and get them at her place. So please do that and thank you very much.

**Former students:**

Dear sir,

How are you and the children? We are still well here at home and also our parents and grandparents.

We are going to school here and there's a new school with two classrooms. There are two teachers here. Our teacher the beginner up to three and the other four to eight. Our teacher's name is Mr. Howes and the other is Mr. Davidson.

We are having trouble in seeing in the school and we are asking if you could sent us our glasses. We would be very happy to learn quicker in class. Say hello to the staff and the girls for us and tell them we miss them all God Bless all of you.

Sincerely,

**Former student:**

Dear Mr. Robinson,

I thought I'd write and tell you that we are doing fine and that I hope your family and all those children you have are fine also.

I suppose the children are getting excited about Christmas by now. Well, I send you my best wishes for Christmas and for the new year ahead.

Art Sinclair and I got married on November 27th. We're doing fine, although things are a bit difficult, but we're both happy.

The main reason I wrote was to ask whether or not it is possible for a treaty Indian to sell out of the treaty rights. Art is not a treaty Indian but I guess I still am. So I was wondering if you could help me arrange to sell my treaty rights as I will have no need for it any longer.

My husband has insurance to pay our medical expenses, but as my husband is not a treaty Indian we see no need in I remaining treaty.

I hope you can arrange things for me as soon as possible. Our address in General Delivery, Red Lake, Ontario.

My husband has a steady job at Campbell Red Lake Gold Mines.

I hope to hear from you in the near future and say "hi" to all the staff for me. I also want to thank you and your wife for being such wonderful parents to me while I was there, although sometimes I was a bit difficult. I send you my gratitude and best wishes.

God Bless you all.

Yours truly

**Former student:**

Mr. Robinson

As I have been very busy, I couldn't write any sooner. You see I just arrived here [Toronto] to that address above. It's been very hard to find Room & Board close to school or institute I go to.

During the time I stayed here I was with Rev. Cooper at Maple, Ont. about seventeen miles out of town.

Transportation has been our problem; now, I'm glad it's solved. I'm a few blocks from the Institute of Trades, that is the place I go to.

Right now, I'm fine well taken care of. Doing my studies too, not too difficult.

It is quite a change to the way I was living at Sioux. I hope to finish. We are taking Math, English, Human Relations, Health, but most of the time it's barbering. All in all it's okay.

Did Mary get her hairdressing started yet? I hope she does. It would be some thing if we had barber business of our own. Maybe it's just another dream.

So, I'll close for now. Oh! Please send my belongings to this address.

Thank you!

Sincerely

P.S.
Tell my friends Hello!
Tell them or ask them
to write to me.

Have you the address of the High School Boys at North Bay?

What about Edward Redsky and Stanley Prince?

If you do, please send them to me. Or ask the Agency for them, please.

Thank you, kindly.

# Chapter 11

**Principal Stephen T. Robinson's** daughter, Marie Loewen, has mixed feelings about the two days she and husband Abe spent with a researcher from the Truth and Reconciliation Commission of Canada in July, 2011.

When they were first contacted by researcher Helen Harrison, they were quite suspicious. There had been such a flood of negative stories about the residential schools. "Okay, what does she want?" they asked each other.

They had received a communication from her similar to an email Ms. Harrison had sent to George McMillan on April 26, 2011, in which she said:

"Your article [in *The Presbyterian Record* in 2009] well describes what many former residential school staff have told me in emails, on the phone and in person. They vividly recall their enthusiasm for the work, their dedication to the children and their dismay at hearing so many troubling stories about the schools. This is a perspective the Commission needs to hear and to understand.

"I work in the research unit of the TRC. I am undertaking a special assignment to meet with former residential school staff (or their children) so the Commission can benefit from their unique insight into the operation of the schools. Your article offers a tantalizing glimpse into your experience at Cecilia Jeffrey and I would very much like to hear more."

Here, for your consideration, is the article by Mr. McMillan that was published in the December, 2009, issue of *The Presbyterian Record*.

> I Have a Bible a Very Special Bible! I had the opportunity recently to meet with The Rev. Harvey Self Moderator of the 135th General Assembly in the Kenora Fellowship Centre. Prior to the meeting I got to wondering if this person was in any way related to three people who had presented me with the gift of a bible as a going away present back in 1953. Yes, 56 years ago.
>
> For a moment let's go back in time to 1953 when I was 19 years old, just out of high school and enjoying the rewards of my first job. I was a member of St. John's Presbyterian Church in Toronto where I was an active member of the choir and the Young People's group. It was here at this time that I was presented with the challenge to take up the work of the Presbyterian Church in Canada under the direction of the W.M.S. [Women's Missionary Society] I was asked to use my schooling and trade skills to teach (Manual Training) Industrial Arts at a school many, many miles away from my family and friends.
>
> The school was the Cecilia Jeffrey Indian Residential School in Kenora, Ontario. I had never been further away from home than the cottage on Georgian Bay just outside Collingwood that was always with family and friends. The train ride west on the "Dominion" seemed to last forever, and the sight of Sudbury the next morning out of Toronto was shocking. I raised my window blind to view what looked like a moonscape. Not a green tree or bush to be seen anywhere.
>
> Questions raced through my mind. Why was I doing this? Where was I going? And why was I leaving every person I had ever loved, and known behind me for this new adventure? The bible I had received explained it all and I was ready to face whatever was ahead of me. I also

have a sister [Gladys Ellis] who served as a registered nurse at C.J. School for a time and there are still a few living friends with whom I share this common thread, of serving others on behalf of the Presbyterian Church in Canada.

Recently our dedication and service has come under some severe criticism in the press. I suppose I would not be far off base to use the word tarnished to describe the results of our labor. The entire situation has been painted with a very large brush to include everything and everyone involved in the residential school program and how they were operated.

The result has been that many, like myself, find ourselves in a very unenviable position. Less than honorable, to be sure, but why? At this very same meeting in Kenora recently I heard the story told that described recent relationships with aboriginal peoples were not based on the services rendered, whether it be food at a catered luncheon or some other service, rather it was people showing their concern for their fellow man that made the difference. That is what cements the bond between individuals.

Somehow this connection with people who tried to make a difference and cared about what they were doing in the residential school system was lost along the way.

What words best describe the feelings and the hurt of those of us who remain? Abandoned? Betrayed? Neglected? For some there is a festering hurt as a result of being lumped into what at times sounds like a cesspool of abuse and cruelty. With no apparent healing process being mentioned or directed towards their plight some remain bluer over the events of recent times.

There was a time when we could look back through photographs and see all the smiling faces enjoying the hockey teams, the trips, the fun and games to name but a few of the activities that kept staff and students at

C. J. School for the most part healthy and well looked after. Those days are gone forever and the good times and lasting life skills that were experienced by so many have been very effectively erased.

Getting back to my bible, the opening page has written in it:

> "'To George McMillan Cecilia Jeffrey School Kenora Ontario
> "Study to shew thyself approved unto God, a workman that needeth not to be ashamed, rightly dividing the word of truth."
> "'II Timothy 2:15.
> "'With Christian Love:
> "'Grace A. Self
> "'Christine G. Self
> "'Stanley D. Self'

On Friday, September, 11th 2009, I was able to ask Harvey if he recognized the signatures on the front of my bible. His response was "I do, they are my parents and my aunt Grace!'" He quickly made a copy of the page and could hardly wait until he would get home so he could show it to his mother. One could say that it was people like these and the message to me on the front page of my bible that set my course for Kenora and here I shall stay.

After 33 years of successfully teaching Industrial Arts I am now retired as my story winds down. In closing I have to say that it is what is written in the pages beyond the "presentation script" that keeps my spirits and my faith strong in spite of the bad press we have to contend with as the saga of the Indian Residential Schools continues.

\* \* \*

When I asked Mr. McMillan in 2020 about his meeting with Ms. Harrison in July, 2011, he had only a dim recollection of the details but did say that she seemed to have had her mind made up before the interview started.

Abe and Maria Loewen wound up feeling pretty much the same way.

When Ms. Harrison first contacted them, she said there were two sides to every coin and she had been given a mandate by the TRC to make sure both sides were covered.

"I want to hear the other side of it," Ms. Loewen quoted her saying.

They took her at her word and, with some reservations, decided to let her come to their home in Kenora. "I wanted Mom and Dad's voices to be heard," Ms. Loewen told me.

However, as with Mr. McMillan, it soon became clear that the TRC researcher came to the table with preconceived ideas about Cecilia Jeffrey Indian Residential School.

"She asked a lot of pointed questions," Ms. Loewen said. "How many children died? Where were they buried? What diseases did they have?" They told her it was their understanding that a boy who died from meningitis back in 1938 was the only student who had died at the school.

"I told her lots of stuff about the children," Mr. Loewen said. "She said she loved hearing the stories. They were all positive. I had no reason to believe her report would be one-sided.

Ms. Harrison spent several hours with them over two days. Before she left, they gave her copies of many of the positive letters students and parents had written during the time Ms. Loewen's father was principal.

As he was driving her to the airport after the last extensive interview, Mr. Loewen said he could write a book about the many good things that had happened at the school.

"I would like to read that," he quoted Ms. Harrison saying, "but it wouldn't make any difference."

That might explain why not a single word of the two days she spent with Abe and Marie Loewen, or from any of the positive letters, made its way into the TRC report.

"She had a preconceived idea of how things were at C.J.," Mr. Loewen told me. "She wasn't interested in anything that didn't fit that negative conception."

Another explanation can be found on Page 230 of historian J. R. Miller's *Residential Schools and Reconciliation* which was published by University of Toronto Press in 2017.

"Although the commissioners frequently said they wanted to hear from school staff and other non-Native peoples as well as former students," Mr. Miller wrote, "the oral record that the commission collected was composed overwhelmingly of survivors' statements.

"Indeed, the professional historian on the TRC staff [Helen Harrison] said that the commissioners' actions 'were not consistent with its claims to wish to include non-Aboriginal voices on the record.'

"Indeed, her budget for the project on school staff was cut from $100,000 to $10,000 and she was told that the Commission would not transcribe the interviews she had conducted. Thus, very few former staff came forward to speak publicly."

A section on Charlie Wenjack in the TRC's report says: "On October 16, 1966, twelve students ran away from the school. Three of the boys walked thirty-one kilometres, reaching the house of a Mr. Benson. He gave them food and let them sleep on the floor.

"The next morning, they made their way to the uncle of two of the boys, Charles Kelly. They were joined that morning by one more of the runaways, another nephew of Kelly's."

The TRC report then makes the same mistake as coroner Dr. R. Glenn Davidson by claiming that Charlie left Mr. Kelly's cabin on Wednesday, October 19, 1966, and headed for home.

"On October 19, after Kelly took his three nephews trapping, the remaining boy, Charlie Wenjack, continued on towards his parents' home at Ogoki Post in the Marten Falls First Nation in Ontario," the report said.

In fact, as we know from what Charles Kelly said in the *Maclean's* article, Charlie didn't leave until the morning of Friday, October 21st, after spending a day and a night at the cabin on the trapline.

Ian Adams' article in *Maclean's* provides a detailed account of him being there until Mr. Kelly turned him loose on the morning of Friday the 21st.

The Notes section of the TRC report refers to the *Maclean's* article three times. If one of the $60 million Commission's researchers had read the article, they would have found the conflict between what Charles Kelly told the inquest jury and what he told Ian Adams.

# Chapter 12

**HERE ARE A** few more letters from parents that were found among the more than 300 positive letters Principal Stephen T. Robinson had collected over the eight fruitful years he and his wife Agnes served at Cecilia Jeffrey Indian Residential School.

I have no doubt that he sent and received a great many more. However, no other letters from students and parents were found among his personal possessions.

**Father:**

> Dear Sir:
>
> We like to apologize for our kids in on time for school. I realize the importance of abiding your school rules but certain conditions of living so remotely makes travelling and transportation difficult.
>
> I am certain the kids will do some real hard school work to catch up for lost time.
>
> Will you look into Peggy's foot. She seems to have pain on her right toe.
>
> Thank you,
>
> Yours truly,

**Father:**

Dear Mister Robbinson,

    Just a few lines to tell you that my son Albert (withheld) will not come home for Christmas as we are out of money right now.
    So try to send us something.
    What my son got for Christmas.
    That will make me happy as my son stays at school so take care of him as we are preying for him to be good.

Sincerely

**Father:**

Dear Mr Stephen t Robinson C.J. school.

>I get your letter today
>Very good Shirley in school
>And I goin up trapping to Eltrut Lake.
>And all fine my boys
>and Shirley mony $3.00
>By candy
>And place next letter
>Mine Centre
>You right keep Shirley [withheld]

From

**Mother:**

Dear Sir,

    I am very sorry that Esther came home when I wasn't expecting her.
    Anyway I am going to send her back its that Greene girl that is trying to come all time.
    Esther likes to go to school.
    I want her to go back.
    She is girl that wouldnt ever answer back when you say anything and one thing I don't let her to go with other girls that runaround. She says Rosella herself wanted to go back
    I guess they were afraid.
    I would like you to ask the Nurse if she can do something about Esther's face.
    It looks worse then it was before.
    Well, I must close. My Delores [withheld] is still in the St. Joseph's Hospital. She will be there in maybe two weeks yet. So maybe you could drive Esther for a visit
    If you have time, like on Sunday evening.

**Father:**

Dear Sir

    I'm sending the kids back to school on time. I noticed yesterday when I brought Danny home he appears to have a little cold. I asked him what was wrong. He said that Terry Green is always pulling him around the collar. He sometimes puts a string around his neck when they line up. I spoke to Jerry about that yesterday. He said that he caught him once doing that.

But Danny and the other boys are scared to say anything because if they went to you and report that, the older boys would always get after them again.

So I would appreciate very much if you would do something about it because I don't want Danny or Cecilia to run away from school. I want my kids to keep on going to school so they can get a better education and better future, but if somebody is going to push them around or be unkind to them, they going to get discouraged. They won't want to go back to school. They like going to school now and we're glad they have nice clothes. So if you check-up on Danny he might have a temperature he seems to be coughing more frequently all day.

So I'll close now and thank you.

**Mother:**

Dear Sir,

I would like to write a brief note to you to-night, to tell you how happy I am to have had Sandra home for the week-end. I want to thank you for permitting her to visit us. I appreciate it very much.

She tells me that you are very kind to them. I thank you for that too.

I will close now with my very best regards to your wife and your child.

Bye for now.
From

**Same mother:**

Dear Sir,

I have given much thought to what I am about to say, this is not on the spur of the moment decision.

I have decided to keep Sandra here at home, rather than have the rest of the school children loose their privilege of going to town. She would be of course be blamed by all if she continued to stay on in school.

I would like to mention at this time too, that I did not sign any form of an application when she entered C.J. School on Oct 16th.

She would run away again anyway if she went back, and I would not like that to happen as she might freeze, because she does not dress warm enough.

You as principal of C.J. School, did not have anything to do with Sandra's running away. She speaks well of you.

This is all.

From

**Temporary parents:**

Dear Mr. Robinson.

Rec'd your letter when we returned from the beach. We have certainly enjoyed having Carol this summer. She is a very sweet girl & it was a pleasure to have her. She fitted into our family so well. When my daughter & her family came home they all loved Carol & she loved them. I think it was good for Carol too for a family of three children raise lots of problems & she was such a help to us all. When she starts out for herself she will know something of the joys & troubles of a family. When they went back to Cleveland she missed them as much as the rest of us.

I have consulted Carol as to what she wants to do about going to Chesley. I told her she could stay till the group [spending the summer with two staff members] go back or go to Chesley & join the group there. She says she would like to stay here for awhile & then go on to join the girls at Chesley. So you can make your plans & then let us know when she will go on & join the girls. So we will wait till you let us know how she will get there.

We would like very much to have Carol come to us at Christmas if that can be arranged. It is a thought & if you think she can come let us know.

We will be pleased to hear from you later.

Sincerely,

**Father:**

Dear Sir

Please let me know if you want to let me have my children soon and my son Albert is gone to Kenora to day. Policeman took him.

If he's in there in your school please ask about him, Margaret and Mary to ask him before they send him if they don't put in your school

Thats what Im asking you to let me have my children soon because I don't like to stay all by my self. They took William Thomas and Albert. They got Pinch drinking.

Yours truly

**Father:**

Dearest Sir,
   We saw your letter about not sending our child back to school. We are very sorry to hear that. She was only here one week. After one week she went back to Red lake to get back to school. That was on Christmas. If she is not back to school, write to Stanly Fiddler at Red Lake. He was going to send her back. If she is back or not write to us again so we'll know.

Sincerely,

**Mother:**

Dear Sir,

   I appreciate writing to me how the schoolchildren are doing at their school work. I often think of my children how they're getting along at school. Hope the Christmas examinations were good especially Edward, Colleen, Marion. Hope they keep up they're school work. When I used to go to school I never thought of going home for holidays especially when it's hard at winters. Heard the children had the measles. Hear to had the measles. Hope their health has been good.
   I was going to write to you earlier to tell you I was not going to take my kids home for holidays as very hard hear, especially when I don't have nobody to support us. I'm all alone and youngest boy is four years old. It's not very long for summer holidays. It's not very long ago when they lost their dad. Edward had a hard time. He just ask me he wanted to go to school, but I know now he likes school. He said they had a gentleman good principal very kind to us he said. I appreciate it very much. I'm asking you a big favour.

Could you possible help us some used clothing. I have a son could send some thing for us, especially two or three blankets. [Illegible] about two summers ago, but never had the chance to go there. We don't have nothing right now. The nurse at Indian agent will be coming up here soon on Jan. 11. Maybe you could drop few things for us clothing she said she be up here on this date. You could take it at the Parsons Airlines or at Indian office that's if you things over I will appreciate if you do. I would not bother if I had somebody to help us. I guess that would be all until now.

Say hello to Edward, Colleen, Marion for me tell them mom is fine and Dennis.

Bye Bye.

Yours very truly

[Women at the Presbyterian churches used to provide home-made quilts, diapers and nighties for babies, blankets and other items that would be shipped to the school and distributed to needy families on the reserves.

[The letters from parents show repeated requests for clothing which would quite often be sent with the children when they returned home for their holidays.]

**Father:**

Dear Sir,

Received your most welcome letter to tell me that you don't mean to keep the children there all the time. Try to understand I really didn't take my son Solly to join the Air Cadets. But I'm getting to realize how fool I am to try and stop him. Like last week, there was a plane leaving here with some kids to play hockey with Red Lake pupils and the plane had a crash and the kids got all killed. That's the reason why I don't want my son to drive a plane. There's lots of things he could do instead of joining Air Cadets.

I didn't let him go to school because want him earn money. But learn something and to know the ways of Jesus Christ our Lord. I showed your most welcome letter to other parents. I mean the parents who have their children joining Air Cadets too and they appreciate it too which I did too. I'm sure you're proud of me I always let three of my children go to school every year. We have a church here and we pray for our children and asking God to bless you for keeping our children happy and healthy which they look like when they come back to us. And one thing more. Since I let my children to school I never receive their [Illegible]and I'm poor and I'm expecting [Rest illegible.]

With everything<br>Yours truly

Merry Christmas

**Parents:**

Dear Principal at C.J.

 We are truely glad to hear from you to know how the children are doing over there.
 We are asking you to send us some of the pictures of the children in school so we may see them. How they are doing.
 Pictures of Laurie Jane and Moses [withheld] and the other children too at their partys, bed times, at the concerts,

play times, meal time, working and at their hockey games when they are in bands and when they are in the classrooms and others too.

I don't mean slides or moving pictures just plain pictures. Let them colored. We're be truely thankful if you sent them to us.

We will pay you if you want it too just tell us how much it costes and we will sent the money to you.

We wish you happy Christmas and happy new year.

We are glad that our Lord Jesus Christ has born on Christmas Day.

May the Lord keep you and to help you to guide the children.

Thanks a lot.

Yours truly

**Father:**

Dear Sir

Here I am writing to you just to let you know we are doing fine and also my family. And I am coming back from my trapline yesterday. And I also give thanks to God. And I also thinking at you and my son and also the other kids that are in school over there. And God will give thanks to your work also. And I want you to tell Richard to write to me because he never write to me yet. And please tell me if he hasn't got the write-pad or envelopes. And I want to tell you I want all my kids to have something to learn what they are learn three of my kids went out to school. One to North Bay and one to Red Lake to. So good-bye. May Glad less you all both of us.

Good-bye

**Parents:**

Dear Sir

Here I am writing to you just writing to you to let you know that we are all still fine her so far we like to here from you again when you see my letter. I can't write very good. I was not in school very longer. I was only in school for five years and Celia my daughter has not write to me yet since the month of Nov. so tell Celia to write to me. And I want you to tell me what grade is she. And I always thanking God to give thanks to you. She was in school here for three years. She did not know anything and I am glad to here from her.

That all for now. So long and good-bye. May God bless you.

**Father:**

Dear Sir,

I am so glad to hear from you. Since Ennis went away this is the first time I hear from him and I'm sure glad to hear that he does what he's told to do. And I also saw the letter that you wrote to me before Christmas. I was so happy to hear about what to say I mean about God to talk about you said. I also pray for you every day to take care of the children that are at school. Tell Ennis to write to us. He never write to us we always write to him.

May God bless you.

Sincerely

**Father:**

Dear Friend,

I receive your letter. Thank you for your letter that I receive.

I am glad to hear that my son Peter is fine and well! Iam sending him $5.00 of money. And I will be sending him again at Christmas.

We are all well here at [withheld].

Please send me my son's picture so I can see him.

I am again glad to hear all the children are well and they are starting school.

I will be writing to you again and I will write to my son too.

I hope some one will read it for him.

May God bless you.

Yours truly,


**Mother:**

Mr. S. Robinson
Principal, C.J. School

Dear Sir,

Would you help us in getting our children back to school.

Would you arrange to send a plane to Windigo Island on the 2nd of January. We will pay you back promptly. If you want, maybe arrangements could be made through the Indian Agency.

In any case, we have no means of sending them back ourselves. I'd hate to see them out of school as they all like it there. We didn't want to leave them at the school when most of the children had gone home.

Mail is very hard to get as we just get it Tuesdays and Fridays. So I won't expect an answer except to watch for a plane. If this is impossible our children will be quite late to school.

Thanking you I remain

Yours truly,

**Grandfather:**

To Steven Robinson,

I am writing a letter to you. I want Solomon to visit me at Christmas time. Because I want to see him. Solomon is my grandson. I wish I could to see all my grandson. I am always thinking about grandson. I never forget him.

That's all for now.

**Brother:**

Dear Principal

We are sending you the bead work you asked for and we want you to give Chris what you want to send up when she comes back home and tell Chris that her sisters are all doing fine and her little brother is fine. I guess that will be all for now. Hope to hear from you soon.

Love

**Parents:**

In an answer to your note concerning Alex's absence from school.
 We have already sent him in and he promised to work hard in his studies. And before Christmas in his examinations he did very well. So I sincerely hope he makes good progress. So we the parents were to blame in not sending him back earlier. Alex is gone back to C.J. School.

That is all
Trhank you.


**Father:**

Dear Principal

 Just a few lines to let you know would you please let me know if Danie [withheld] received any money from Indian Affairs Selkirk Man. $5.00 her treaty money [Illegible.] that before her holidays last year.

Thank you.
Yours truly,


**Father:**

Dear Sir,

 I was not able to do any commercial fishing as I am laid up with a couple of fractured ribs. I was under Dr. Leckie's care.

I will repay you as immediate as possible when I get motivated again. I am very anxious to see these kids go back and not miss so much school and when they are doing so well.

Thank you.

**Mother:**

Dear Mr. Robinson,

Just want to ask you if you know the address of Mr. Donald Stevens. We sure would like to know their address.
The one that Violet [Withheld] was invited by.
Violet is doing just fine in school. She's very happy to go to school with her sister every day. Also, she's fine. Just a little cold this winter.
It's very cold in [Withheld]. The coldest weather we have so far.
I'm very thankful for all of you staff members. The way you treat the children also to my daughter.

Best regards

# Chapter 13

**SHORTLY BEFORE HIS** death at the age of 80, after a sudden heart attack, in May, 1992, Stephen T. Robinson drafted a letter to the editor of the *Presbyterian Record* in response to an article about Cecilia Jeffrey Indian Residential School with a headline that said "No Clean Hands."

The subhead read: "Former residents of Presbyterian residential schools report abuses similar to those found elsewhere."

The article was based on the transcript of an interview the editor had conducted with Rev. Ray Hodgson, General Secretary for Church and Society; Rev. Ian Morrison, General Secretary of Board of Canada Operations for the Board of World Mission; and June Stevenson, editor of *Glad Tidings*.

The trio had been in Kenora in July, 1991, where they interviewed eight former students, Stephen T. Robinson, his wife Agnes and former nurse Kay Blake.

At the time of the interview, Cecilia Jeffrey Indian Residential School had been closed for 15 years.

On July 19, 1991, Ms. Stevenson, who was harshly critical of Cecilia Jeffrey in the interview with the editor of the *Presbyterian Record*, wrote a letter to Stephen and Agnes Robinson in which she said:

Dear Mr. & Mrs. Robinson,

Thank you so much for taking the time to meet with Ian, Ray and myself, and especially to show us your slides. It helped a great deal to picture life at CJS.

I would appreciate receiving some pictures, either slides or prints, however you are able to send them: K.P. [kitchen patrol] Duty, Scouts, View of the School, Hockey players, the farm at Birtle [In addition to Cecilia Jeffrey, the Presbyterian Church operated a school in Birtle, Manitoba.], Girls choir in Montreal. These will add immensely to my article for Glad Tidings, later in the year.

I would encourage you also to prepare your pictures, etc. for the Archives. If I can help in any way, let me know.

**Thanks also for sharing the letters** [emphasis added]. They gave us an insight into the daily life with all its challenges and difficulties on both sides—at home and school. **They are a fond testimony to your time at CJS** [emphasis added].

I will be in touch again.<br>
Sincerely,<br>
*June*<br>
L. June Stevenson

Not a word about what Mr. and Mrs. Robinson had said about life at Cecilia Jeffrey made it into the interview with the editor of the *Presbyterian Record*. Nor was there any mention of former nurse Kay Blake. It was a complete hatchet job.

On reading the article in the *Presbyterian Record*, Mr. Robinson felt a profound sense of betrayal. He and his wife Agnes had agreed in good faith to be interviewed by Rev. Ray Hodgson, Rev. Ian Morrison and Ms. Stevenson.

They had been given no indication during the interviews that the trio would be so scathing in their criticism of the school.

He drafted a letter to the editor responding to pretty much everything they had gotten wrong about the Indian residential school into which he had poured eight years of his life.

For some reason, however, he decided not to send it.

The letter was found along with the more than 300 positive letters from students and parents he had received during his eight years as principal of Cecilia Jeffrey Indian Residential School.

This is the letter he drafted.

Editor;

For some time I have been intending to make some reply to the article "No Clean Hands" that appeared in the February issue of the Record I considered it to be a political reply to a political accusation.

These days it is in order to blame everyone from Columbus down for the plight of the Native people. I had hoped that our people could have responded with some of the positive things that were done instead of the condemnation of the whole system. The title and most of the interview were of a tabloid nature and certainly not worthy of our own church paper.

The paragraph charging the church of quick assimilation into the lowest rungs of European society. Every means to break the spirits and make them pliable and amenable to that assimilation was taken.

This is an accusation against the whole church and should have been challenged in the courts of the church. In our system of church government the courts of the church speak. Not even the Moderator of the Assembly has this right.

The better part of the [Indian residential school] system was to assist them in becoming vocal and provide them with the skills that would prepare them to compete in the larger society. This has been accomplished to a degree in that many former students are now in places of leadership. Nearly all the Chiefs in the Kenora area are former Residential School students.

The people interviewed met with a former student who is the Director of the [Indigenous] Sacred Circle family services. A minister of our church is a former student. If I had the Presbyterian Sharing budget at my disposal I could give scores of former students in the Northern Reserves. Scores who are now teachers, social workers, language coaches and many good parents who are still in touch with us.

"Incoherent rage" supposedly experienced by one of the persons must have blinded his eyes and deafened his ears to some of these things. Some were related in the December issue of the Glad Tidings. Why did these people not relate them to the wider readership of the Record? They came out of an interview with three people.

I would say to the Secretary of Justice that incoherent rage, powerful emotions, are not conducive to the fulfilling of the task the church has entrusted to him. In the halls of Justice there is displayed a scale that balances the pros and cons of a matter. All were condemned. Even the Apostle Paul was quoted. A quotation that is general in nature and could be applied to the interviewed and also to the article in general.

The girls choir we took to Montreal in 1964 was a great credit to the school and the church. The awards won at the local music festival were a credit to the children and the teachers. Many were in spoken poetry as displayed in the tape enclosed. The trophy for spoken poetry was donated in memory of a former nurse at the school. Just two weeks ago one of the choir girls requested a copy of the tape to share with her daughter and grand-daughter.

A former student was director of a local Aboriginal family services agency.

We have powerful emotions when a former student comes and says "I am now a Christian" or another when questioned about pow-wows says "we go to the [Christian] tent meetings." When former students from Shoal Lake greet you with "so and so is not drinking any more he comes to our meetings all the time."

We would remind the secretary [Rev. Ray Hodgson] that Jesus did figure in our theology. A quote from one of these people who now conduct some of their own services "we now know what you taught us at C.J."

My wife and I went to C.J. in response to a call from the church, we accepted it as a gospel call. Where we have erred we are so relieved that God will be our judge and not our Christian friends. Our deeds are not recorded at 50 Wynford Drive [Head office of the Presbyterian Church in Canada].

My only regret is that the names of many saintly people have been tarnished and how do you erase that from the minds of your readers?

I am now in my thirty-fourth year in Kenora. I cherish the memory of many people I have known and (even dug graves). The C.J. cemetery is full of people who for some reason are there because their loved ones chose that resting place rather than the one on the reserve. WHY?

I am proud that when I attend my church (which would not be there if there had not been a C.J.) I view a window (St. Peter) dedicated in honor of the staff and students of C.J. school.

I am also saddened when daily I meet the street people and wonder how to minister to them. All one can do is to acknowledge them as souls for whom Christ died and take time to talk to them. And they do quite often ask for prayer.

In considering the history of the Christian church it is noted that it very often pioneered in various fields, hospitals, education, and in social work. Was there really a conspiracy with the government to break the spirits of these people? Or did those people have a vision of what lay ahead for a people not prepared for the onslaught of a new society and the depletion of the livelihood they had known for centuries? Was the ability to communicate a necessity for their survival? Is this not what our church had in mind?

With the closure of the old Indian House situated in Anishinabe park another venture of our church was the establishment of the K.F.C. (Kenora Friendship Centre). This centre was one of the first of many centres to operate in Ontario.

The Director of the centre was the secretary of the Federation of centres for 4 years. The charter for the organization was drawn up at K.F.C. and it was mainly by the promptings of the K.F.C. representative on the federation that the Nee-Chee Indian Centre was recognized and funded. K.F.C. was never funded by the Government.

Here again the church pioneered and must withdraw now that need does not exist. The building is now empty. Where are the people who are so quick to condemn the past and then as they put it "we need to tie it [Apology and confession] into specific actions." Could some of these actions take place in that empty building?

One more positive thing about former students. The Indian House was operated by a student from the old school at Shoal Lake. His son who was given a job at K.F.C. (also a former student) was with his wife in charge of a program for recovering alcoholic [Indigenous] women. This Water St. Residence program was later renamed Clarissa Manor and is fully government funded. Another program started by the church.

We could tell of the many times the school and the Centre have been a haven for battered [Indigenous] people and homeless children. They will not be found in the [Presbyterian] Archives for they were considered a part of the love and compassion expected of those who were "called." Of course the others have been amply described.

I hope I have not burdened you with this other side but I could not help but do it in behalf of those were not quite as dirty.

Of course, your readers will never hear this other side but then those people did not seek publicity or a picture in the Record.

Your brother in Christ

Stephen T. Robinson

c.c. Chairman Board of Missions
Principal Clerk of Assembly
Ian Morrison

\* \* \*

In an article that was published in *Historical Papers 1993, Canadian Society of Church History*, Peter Bush, who would become Moderator of the Presbyterian Church in Canada in 2018, wrote: "Barbara Dean became the teacher of the senior class at the [Presbyterian] Birtle [Indian Residential] school [in Birtle, Manitoba.] in September 1946, and quickly realized that if she was going to teach effectively she would have 'to have respect for Indian culture.'

"Towards this purpose she tried to obtain dictionaries of Sioux, Cree and Saulteaux (the three languages spoken by the Native children at Birtle School) as well as a book of Indian songs and ceremonial dances.

"This openness to Native culture was reflected in the work of J. Eldon Andrews, principal of Cecilia Jeffrey 1952-1953, who resurrected a student government system that had been introduced by E. W. Byers in the 1930s.

"The student government was built on the Native model of an Elected Chief and Band Councillors—thus within the confines of the school, the council and chief had self-government.

"Andrews argued that anyone working with the Native people of Canada had to have a solid understanding of sociology and anthropology, further he maintained that teachers and administrators at Cecilia Jeffrey School should learn Ojibwa as a pre-requisite to teaching Native children English."

It is also worth noting that Rev. Bush said extensive research that he had conducted uncovered only one incident of severe abuse at Cecilia Jeffrey Indian Residential School between 1925 and 1969.

The incident involved a Mr. Pitt who became principal of the school in 1944. Given the nature of the abuse, it is worth quoting Rev. Bush at length.

"[Elizabeth W.] Byers' replacement, Pitts, was a strict disciplinarian who believed in the use of the strap. The following was reported in the WMS-WD [Women's Missionary Society Western District] by a Miss Ross, a teacher at Cecilia Jeffrey.

> ...one time when the children were being strapped ... from the noise it seemed as if the girls were being knocked against the wall. A rubber strap is used which must reach the children's arms because they swell. The door opened and it seemed as though someone tumbled out. Mr. Pitts called out "You dirty, filthy" but Miss Ross did not catch the last word. "Spit it out in the hall, you dirty, lying rats," he concluded.

"On another occasion Mr. Pitts had called the children in Miss Ross' classroom 'You dirty, lying sneaks."

"Ross also noted that Pitts had beaten a boy so badly that he had to be cared for by the nurses. The WMS-WD executive took Ross' complaints under advisement but the minutes of the meeting held with her by the WMS-WD executive show little concern over Pitts' disciplinary style. Ross left the school in April, 1944, saying she could no longer work in that kind of environment."

Rev. Bush found evidence of "sexual immorality" at Cecilia Jeffrey back in the late 1930s.

"[I]n 1939 the Indian Affairs Branch and the Ontario Provincial Police (OPP) visited Cecilia Jeffrey School, following up rumours of sexual immorality among students and between students and staff, and to pursue charges regarding the misappropriation of government funds.

"The OPP took statements from fifteen young people in their mid-teens who had engaged in heterosexual intercourse in the dormitories and on the grounds of the school. The students' statements made reference to their witnessing some of the unmarried staff engaging in sexual activity.

"One student, age seventeen, stated that he had been seduced by the supervisor of the girls' dormitory.

"None of these statements were ever followed up by the police or by the WMS-WD. The only result of the investigation was that it provided further grounds for the removal of Byers (who had been resisting orders from Indian Affairs) as principal of the school."

In summing up the state of affairs at Cecilia Jeffrey Indian Residential School during that period, Rev. Bush said: "It seems clear from the two situations recounted above that Cecilia Jeffrey was struggling under poor leadership through the period from 1937 to 1945. The leaders created an atmosphere in which physical abuse was able to exist unchecked.

"But these are the only examples of this type of abuse that my research has discovered."

# Chapter 14

**THIS IS THE** final batch of letters written by parents between 1958 and 1966.

**Mother:**

>Mr. S. Robinson
>Cecilia Jeffrey School
>Kenora Ontario
>Box 130

>Dear Sir:

>I decided to drop a few lines so you know I'm still living, hope your okay too and I'm saying hello to Agnes, your wife and I'm a picture of me, see the different.
>This is my mother(?) letter down here. I would like you to give my children some clothing because I don't have enough money to buy them clothes. That's why I'm asking you.

>From

**Father:**

Dear Sir

Just a line to you. Want to know if my son Jackson [withheld] is still alive. I haven't heard from him in a long time or is he in some other school or if he's at C.J. I'd be very glad to know if he is well and happy and tell him to write to me enclosed is a letter to him give to him and forward it to wherever he may be. This is it for now.
Awaiting your reply.
God bless you all at C.J.
Thank-you.

Sincerely,

**Mother in sanatorium:**

Dear Principal

Just a few lines to ask you, how is my daughter Linda Mae [withheld]? Hope she's fine. She wrote to me last month and she told me she's going to sneak away from there in the spring time. I'm so worried about her ever since she told me about it.
Please don't let her go to town. Could you please send me the Bible. I need it.
Concluding with best of luck to you. Hope t hear from you.

Thanks.

Sincerely

I am doing fine so far.

## On behalf of potential student:

Dear Mr. Robinson;

    I wrote the Anglican Indian Residential School Sioux Lookout regarding a Johnny [withheld], Johnny wants in the worst way to go to school and is a very ambitious boy, he has finally won the consent of his foster parents to get started and I want to do all I can to help him get started. Johnnys No. is 402. Mr. Barrington of the Sioux Lookout School wrote to me and informed me that their school was filled to capacity and suggested that I write to you as it was possible that you might have a vacancy.
    I would appreciate hearing from you as soon as possible as Johnnys parents Pat and Rosie [withheld.] will be leaving the camp October 5th for their Trap Line on Bruce Lake and I would like to assist Johnny get lined up before that time. Any assistance you can give me will be greatly appreciated. Johnny has been at the camp with us for five summers and I can say he is one of the nicest Indian Boys I have come in contact with.

Very truly yours,

## Mother:

Dear Mr. Robinson,

    I am so glad that my little girl Violet is in school now cause you are taking good care of her cause I can't look after her.
    This is all I'm going to say to you. Please write to us how she's doing or if she doing or if she good or bad.

Bye Bye

**Father:**

Dear Sir,

Ernest doesn't like being pick on when he just stands around the boys pick on him and I don't like that. You should be responsible for that. That's why Ernest didn't go to school. That's why they ran away, if my son runs away that means that the boys pick on him and make him cry. So you better tell the boys to behave themselves. If he tells me again I'm going to send him to a different school.

Yours truly,

**Father:**

Dear Teacher

I had seen your letter you wrote to me. And I "thank you" very much for telling me how Mary is. And that she's eating well. She doesn't eat anything she only eats when we gave her something to eat. She doesn't like anything and we would like you to tell us how she is sometimes. We think of her all the time. We love her very much.

All for now.

**Father:**

Dear Sir

I saw your letter which you wrote to me the last time too and I was very happy to hear everything. How they eat too. Were going to send our son [Illegible] agin. We can't go and see our children because its to far away and we are happy that your looking after our son good.

God bless you.

From

**Father:**

Mr. Robinson,

We are enclosing a check of $10.00# which will be for there (Donnie & Shirley) bus fare and the rest that will be left-over will be for stuff the want to buy for Easter, and I'll meet them at the bus-depot here in Fort Frances when they come in.

We are doing fine here, hope it's the same with you & wife & your daughter.

Thank you.<br>Yours Truly

**Father:**

Dear principal,

I am asking how much the train or bus fares would cost for children like Ian and Daisy from Kenora to Sioux Lookout. How much does it cost in one way, and in the return trip? We would like if our children could come home, but I'm not quite sure whether or not if they are coming. Do the parents pay for both trips? Do you let the children from the far North have their holidays earlier, who are going home on their Christmas holidays.

When do they usually start their Christmas holidays and when do they start back to school? How many days do they have holidays. I was wondering whether they could come home on Christmas. If the fares arent too high I will send for them, I'm already saving some money. I have already asked the areoplane fares.

Their Mom was out to Sioux Lookout to have a baby when they were having their summer holidays, been away for almost a month. She would like to see them again. Please, answer my letter soon.

Yours truly

**Father:**

Mr Robinson

    Both me and my wife agree to let our daughter work for Dr. Torrie.
    All of us are OK out here
    Powassins are fine too.
    I hope our children are getting along fine at school.

Thanks for writing.

**Father:**

Dear Sir,

    I am sending a money order of $11.70 for the fare that Ennis (withheld) to visit us on his Easter Holiday.
    Can you tell me about what time he will get to Red Lake on Friday April 12$^{th}$?
    I mean what time he will arrive?

And when he returns to school on Saturday, when is it going to be, in the morning or in the afternoon? You let me know because I don't know anything about Bus Schedules.
Thank you!
I am send the money order separate!

From

**Mother:**

Dear sir,

Here I am dropping a few lines just to let you know we are still all fine and I am very sorry I did'nt answer you most welcome letter and I was thankful to here from you and to here your very nice story about there food
Ill asked daugher about you mention to me about high school.
Please send me Celia (withheld) picture
I want to see it
Well that's all for now
Good bye.

From

**Mother:**

Dear Sir,

We saw your letter which you wrote to us, on Feb. 27. And we will very happy if you could write to us once a month And let us know how my little girl Mary is doing at school and if she is feeling well.

We want her to write to us too when you write to us. And we are very happy to hear that they get enough to eat.

Tell Mary not to get any trouble or wandering off from school.

You have our Big Thank You for looking after our little girl Mary so well

My Best Regards.

May God Bless and Keep in a good path

Yours truly

**Mother:**

Dear Sir,

I just want to ask you. How are all my son's. They haven't write to me for long time. May be they are in hospital or not. And I'll be glad if you tell me about them reall soon. And I feel bad cause I never heard from them. I send them some money before so they can write to me. And we send them some things I wand to know if they got those all. Please tell me if those things didnt get to school. And you are to tell if those boys are not doing well. This is all I can say till again. Solong.

**Father:**

Dear Sir

Here I am writing a letter to you once again and let me know did you see my other letter I was write to you at last month and can you send it to me. Picture—for my son and I very happy for you. You will have good keeping to my children. Thank you and please send it to me pictures for Banulas and Joyce [withheld]. That's all. May God bless you.

From

**Father:**

Dear Sir:

    I'm so glad to hear from you. My daughter she doing good.
    I'm thank you very much you tell my Daught she doing fine.
    Please write to us again if you have time.
    Thank you again

Your truly

**Father:**

Dear Sir,

    We will be sending the kids in to Sioux Lookout on Friday Sept. 4. We will be expecting you or the Indian agent to arrange their transportation from Sioux Lookout to Kenora.

yours truly

<u>Children's names</u>
Anna (withheld)
Sally (withheld)
Laura (withheld)

**Mother:**

Dear Stephen,

Let me know soon if anything happens to my boys over there. They have not write for a long time now. It will be more good if you would write and tell me about them.

From,

PS
I got your letter on Dec.

**Father:**

Dear Sir,

We certainly was happy to hear from our daughter, Lydia [withheld], which we are anxious to see her back home soon again. We are all thankful that she is doing fine and well cared. Thank you very much for everything.
I hope you are doing fine just like us. God bless you all and good-bye.

Yours truly,

**Father:**

Sorry I did not answer your letter of January 31st about the suitcase, you can keep it there until next June.
As for Dinah if she does not behave there send her away to a reformatory school or send her home. Both me & the wife do not like her to go the same way as Mary.

If you should send her home let us know in advance so somebody can go and meet her at Sioux Lookout.

Sincerely yours

**Father:**

Dear Sir,

We saw your letter which you wrote to us telling us all about our children. We just filled with joy as we listened to your most welcome letter. I will be happy if you will write to us every month telling us about our children.

We are all doing fine including our daughter Madeline she never gets sick. And we are thankful.

God bless you all.

Yours truly,

**Father:**

Dear friend

I just want to ask you.

How's my son doing. I always thing of you to look after Maida [withheld] and her brother.

And if they doing fine let me know. You can write to me. I always thing of my son. When he's gone. I thing you know him Maida [withheld's] brother.

That's will be all for now. May God bless you always.

**Father:**

Dear Sir

> I want you to let me know how is my little girl.
> I want you write me.
> We going out trapping way north about 24 October.
> We stay there all winter Eltrut Lake
> I get my mail Mine Centre Ont.
> I enclose 5 dollars money order for my daughter. I want you save for her give her some when she want buy something.
> Please write me and tell when school vacation time.

From your friend.


**Father:**

Dear Sir:

> I'm just wandering why you never write to me about Ennis. You never mentioned to me anything about him. Thought I've heard that he has been having some operations. So I wanted you to let me know about him. How he is or what he's doing! And I want to tell you that he might not go back to school next fall. I will be writing for you to let me know how he is because he hasn't written for a long time.
> I always pray for you that you will teach all the children well. And I want you to pray for me as I'm always sick.
> May God bless you always!

From

**Parents:**

Dear Sir

We are very glad to hear from you. We are very happy for letting us know about our children and we are very thankful for taking care of our children.
And we want to ask you one thing if you could take a picture of our daughter Marjorie Martha [withheld] and send it to us please. We didn't have money to let our daughter come home on Christmas we send her a Christmas present on Christmas.

Yours truly,

**Father:**

Dear Friend
I had your letter Dec. 10 to tell you we can't do what you said about kids. Just keep them safe for us and we always pray for you and we always hope that they may not happen something to them. I hope that they pray on Christmas. I guess I will be want them to come home in summer because its to far from here to send them home for Christmas. I guess its better for them to say here all year.
Thank you for your keep them for us.
Thank you very much.
May God bless you a happy merry Christmas to you.

Happy New Year.

**Parents:**

Dear Sir,

I would trouble you to do a favour for me.
Would you please tell my son Jackson [withheld] to write us a letter as we are very anxious to hear from him.
He hasn't written us since he went back to school last Sept. We are anxious to know how he is. But we did here he was in Red Lake on Christmas holidays.

Thank you.
Yours very truly
Mr. & Mrs. [withheld]


**Father:**

Principal Stephen T. Robinson;

I'm not sure if I'm getting this straight. I signed the enclosed from so you could do whatever is necessary if any of my children gets hurt, for instance, broken leg, broken arm and so on.
As for my two daughters who are crippled, I don't want them to get treatment concerning their crippleness. In other words, leave them the way they are.
That's all I have to say.
Take good care of the kids.

Very sincerely,

**Mother:**

ToCecil Jeffrey School
Kenora Ont.

Please advise how my sons Morris, Albert and Charlie are making out. Haven't heard from them for ages.

Yours very truly,

**Mother:**

Dear Sir

I was very glad to hear about my sons and my daughter. Its soon to see them back home. Oh yes I want them & bring back with them with good neat cloths. Give them good cloths when they come home because I haven't money to buy clothes for them. I haven't much money for them to buy shirt and pants so that's why I'm asking you to give them good cloths when they come home. Last summr I had enough money when my sons work with fire. So I will be glad if you do. This is all I can say to you since this is all for now.

**Father:**

Dear Sir

We are very glad that our child is doing good in school and we'd very much appreciate if when ever our child is in need of medical care or dental care I give you full authority and we're very glad today that you're keeping in touch with us about her health and we hope to see her in good health when we see her in the summer and please tell her to write to us. We only received one letter from her. May God bless you and teach you how to guide the children.

Yours truly,

**Father:**

Dear Sir,

I have seen your letter yesterday. I can't come to school to get my childen and I am happy to hear that my children are well. We also are fine. Things here are not like they use to be. Sometime we don't have anything to eat, the reason is because I can't hunt any more.

That's all for now.

**Father:**

Dear Sir

Well am very glad to hear from you and I'm very happy to see a Christmas day. We have a thankful which god give us to see another happy holiday.
 Well just telling you about my boys I can't help them cause it's too far from here. They'll have to use a plane its about 300 miles north from Sioux Lookout and they'll have to take too long. That's the trouble. We have a lot of fur alright but not enough coat. Just enough to buy food to eat. I'll pray for them every time when I pray.

And would you please send its to me a picture of themselfs. I want see them. And be sure and send them on summer. Merry Christmas & and happy new year.

                                                             Yours truly,

**Father:**

Dear Sir:

    I recievered Jackson report and I like it very muck. Tell Jackson to wirte to me I never got a letter from him. Give this to him please I hope they are all doing at school.

                                                             Yours tukely

**Father:**

Dear Friend

    Just thought of dropping you a few lines to you. I received your most welcome letter and I very happy about telling me about my son and Joyce. And I am sending some money for my childs in school. And if you see this my letter that I sending you as I likc to know and if you get the money too tell me. And I send $3 for my childs for immediately thanks and I am still wwriting to send it to me some pictures for my child. Well I guess this is well be all for now. May God bless you.
    Reply if you receive this my letter. Thank you.

                                                         From yours truly,

**Mother:**

Dear Mr. Robinson,

We got the letter you wrote to me and I was very happy to hear from you to tell me that Mary is fine. I'm very happy that she listens to you. And please try to sent a picture of her, we are very anxious to see her.

My family is in a top shape and so are most of the people.

And I want to Thank You for looking after our girl Mary.

My best regards,

God bless you and help you.

Yours truly,

**Father:**

Happy Easter to you
Dear My friend

I'm telling you that I want you to keep them safty for us, I mean my children Emma and Alice. So they may not drowned or some thing. Like thats what I want you to do. Dont let them walk far away. And when they come home, give them something to wear coats and shoes too good ones, because we dont have anything for them because we dont get much furs. Thats why I'm asking you this and send me with big pants and shirts for me.This is all for now. I'm say hello to you my friend.

Thank you, that you'll keep my kids for me and my God bless you all and love us all and keep us all.

**Father:**

Dear Mr. Robinson

    We wanted to tell you how happy we are to hear from you once again. And want to thank you for taking care of them from illness, seeing that they are not sick right now.
    We want them to have a good education so that they may go to high school soon. We don't want Rubma to quit school until she finished her schooling. Tell her to work hard and must concentrate on her school work.
    May God bless you and keep you always.

Sincerely yours,

**Father:**

Dear Sir:

    First of all it is a great pleasure for me to write and talk about my son [withheld]. I told him that we would send for him to visit us at Red Lake for Christmas Holidays so please send him to Red Lake with the other children at Christmas. Also please let us know how he is and how he behaves, if he's a bad boy like stealing and fighting as doesn't do as he's told. He will no longer stay there if he isn't a good boy. Because he's always a good boy when he's home

Yours truly,

**Father:**

Dear Sir

    We are happy to see you letters. And are happy to hear that Nora is doing fine.
    We are saying that Nora is going back to school next year until she finish school.
    On Christmas time we didn't have any money that's why Nora didn't have a holiday.
    God bless you.

Yours truly,

**Father:**

Dear Sir

    I'm very glad the way you have been saying to me on your letter.
    I didn't find any school report enclosed on your letter.
    I'm asking you to send me a picture of "David."

Thank you.

**Parents:**

Dear Sir,

    We are very glad that you told us that our daughter Lydia is doing fine. And also I would be very happy to see her healthy when she comes home. I want her to eat what she needs. And I want you to write to me [illegible] never receive a letter from my dear little girl. I would appreciate that very much.

I'm asking God that I will see my daughter when she comes home.

We are saying "thank you" for writing to us.

Yours truly,

# Chapter 15

THE BOOK ABOUT Charlie Wenjack that is being used in more than 65,000 classrooms across Canada and in the United States paints an altogether darker picture of life at Cecilia Jeffrey Indian Residential School than what we have heard from the former staff and read in the positive letters from students and parents.

Despite the fact the school was operated by the Women's Missionary Society of the Protestant Presbyterian Church in Canada, the book has graphic drawings showing Catholic nuns in habits delousing an emaciated-looking Charlie and other Ojibway boys who are covering their genitals with their hands. A priest with a large white cross on his chest drags a screaming girl across the playground.

Elementary school children reading *Secret Path* see a priest standing in the dormitory doorway as Charlie watches anxiously from his bed. There's a closeup of the priest's crotch followed by a drawing of his hand reaching out for the terrified boy.

Lyrics by the late Gord Downie, lead singer for *The Tragically Hip* rock band, on the opposite page say: "I heard them in the dark. Heard the things they do. I heard the heavy whispers. Whispering, 'Don't let this touch you'."

There is no evidence that Charlie was sexually abused by any member of the staff at Cecilia Jeffrey Indian Residential School, let alone by a pedophile Catholic priest.

There were no nuns or priests at the school. None of the staff wore clerical garb.

The book, which features graphic drawings by illustrator Jeff Lemire and lyrics by Gord Downie, was published by Simon & Shuster Canada in October, 2016, the 50th anniversary of Charlie's death.

The online order form for the book says: "Working with [Gord] Downie's poetry and music, [Jeff] Lemire has created a powerful visual representation of the life of Chanie [Charlie] Wenjack."

The text on the back cover says Charlie died "trying to **escape** [emphasis added] the Cecilia Jeffrey Indian Residential School."

The text also says: "Chanie Wenjack haunts us. His story is Canada's story. We are not the country we think we are. History will be re-written. All of the Residential Schools will he pulled apart and studied.

"The next hundred years are going to be painful and unsettling as we meet Chanie Wenjack and thousands like him—as we find out about ourselves, about all of us—and when we do, we can truly call ourselves 'Canada'."

*Secret Path* is quite clearly meant to be read as a true, and accurate, account of 12-year-old Charlie Wenjack's lonely death. However, by using a real person instead of a composite, they are also saying that all of the abuse he is said to have suffered would have been at the hands of the staff of the school—who are also real people.

If, as would have been more appropriate, they had created a composite figure to represent the children who actually did suffer emotional, physical and sexual abuse in the residential schools, the former staff who cared for the children as if they were their own would not have been as traumatized by the manner in which they are depicted in *Secret Path*.

Let's take a look at the book.

The text on the back cover says Charlie's real name is "Chanie" but the school changed it to Charlie.

Despite considerable research, I could find nothing to substantiate the claim that the school changed Charlie's name from "Chanie" to Charlie.

In fact, his family has always called him Charlie.

When Charlie's older sisters, Pearl Achneepineskum and Daisy Munroe, visited a Grade 5 class at Toronto's Dundas Junior Public School in 2017, a little Chinese-Canadian boy caught Ms. Achneepineskum's attention.

"Here's a little guy that looks like and feels like Charlie, you know," she said with a big smile. "I want to take him home. I don't know if he's going to agree with that. He looks mischievous."

While describing a picture the little boy who reminded her of Charlie had drawn, Ms. Achneepineskum said it showed "Charlie on the railway tracks."

An introductory note accompanying an audiotape of Ms. Achneepineskum being interviewed by the CBC's Carol Off on *As It Happens* on October 20, 2016, said she referred to her brother as "Charlie."

When Charlie's family and relatives show up at special events honoring his memory, they wear blue T-shirts with the name *Charlie* Wenjack embossed on the front.

Charlie's mother died on September 1, 2017, at the age of 89. Her obituary lists him as "Charlie."

The marker on his grave at his home community of Ogoki Post says:

IN LOVING MEMORY
SON
**CHARLES** WENJACK
1954–1966

However, the name "Chanie" is used in the buildings that have been named in his memory, the more than 50 "Legacy Spaces" and in all newspaper, radio and TV reports.

\* \* \*

The cover of *Secret Path* shows a downcast Charlie sitting on one of the swings in the playground at Cecilia Jeffrey Indian Residential

School. There's a big wire fence to the right. The playground is encircled by trees.

At the beginning of the book, there's a drawing of three boys at the swings in the playground. Two sitting and one standing. They're facing the back of the school. That would appear to be Charlie with Ralph McDonald and his brother Jack.

Large fir trees are shown in the background, as if the school had been built in a clearing in the forest. On the right side of the drawing, three boys are shown kicking a ball around beside a high wire fence.

I compared the drawing with photos I had obtained showing the playground at the time Charlie was on the swings.

Looking at the playground from the back of the school, you'd see that it's a wide, expansive, grassy area that eventually slopes down to the shore of Round Lake. There's no evidence of the lake in the drawing. Just a solid forest of trees.

As for the high wire fence, there was no fence there in any of the photos I looked at. It's safe to say that the fence shown in *Secret Path* did not exist.

Students see a priest shaving a despondent Charlie's long black hair with an electric razor, locks drifting down beside his bare feet on the floor. Two unhappy-looking Ojibway boys in blankets stand in front of a locker waiting their turn.

Jeff Lemire's next drawing show nuns in habits delousing an emaciated-looking Charlie and four other Ojibway boys who are covering their genitals with their hands.

A fully-clothed priest is shown watching Charlie and three other boys taking a shower.

The next drawing the children see is a young boy dressed only in pyjama bottoms in the school dormitory yelling in pain as a nun with a big cross hanging from her neck yanks his ear.

There's a drawing of Charlie and four other boys in their beds in the dormitory. Then the children see a picture of Charlie only followed by a closeup of an anxious look on his face.

In a lyric titled *Swing Set,* Gord Downie says Charlie and the McDonald brothers were on the swings at the playground. "Now?" Charlie asked. "Not yet," one of the brothers replies.

Mr. Downie then writes:

> Over the rise in the lawn
> Someone dragging someone
> The kid looking me in the eye
> Teacher not looking at anyone

A drawing by Jeff Lemire a few pages on shows Charlie and the McDonald brothers on the swings watching a priest chasing a young girl across the playground. He catches her, grabs her by the arm and heads for one of the school doors as Charlie and his friends look on.

Again, there were no priests at Cecilia Jeffrey—and some of the real people who **were** there are still alive.

According to *Secret Path*, it was at that point that the boys decided to make a run for it.

Gord Downie's lyrics have Charlie saying:

> I looked around me only once
> Didn't see nobody chasing us
> Just my swing dancing in the sun
> Dancing wildly where it was
> Now?
> Now. Yes
> Now?
> Now. Yes.

That would indicate that it was Charlie who took the initiative to leave the school playground that afternoon. However, as you might recall from the report in the *Kenora Daily Miner and News*, the main reason the boys left that afternoon was because Ralph McDonald had a sudden urge to visit his uncle. Nothing had been planned. The decision was made on the spot.

That is also the way Ian Adams described it in his February, 1967, article in *Maclean's*.

A drawing by Jeff Lemire shows Ojibway students sitting at their desks with expressionless looks on their faces, arms hanging limply at their sides, as if waiting for the priest beside one of the desks to whack them with a big stick.

That's quite a contrast to the way the school is depicted in the positive letters written by students who were there at, or around, the time Charlie was there. It should also be noted that Charlie was attending a public day school at that time.

Children reading *Secret Path* see a drawing of boys and girls with their hands held in prayer at a chapel with a nun at the back of the chapel and one at the front reading from the Bible.

Again, there were no nuns or priests at Cecilia Jeffrey Indian Residential School.

Charlie watches anxiously as a priest stands beside his bed in the dormitory. The priest steps closer.

Later in *Secret Path*, there's a drawing of a man outside a cabin with two young boys standing in front of him. This would appear to be the McDonald brothers' uncle, Charles Kelly, with whom Charlie and his three young friends stayed from Monday morning until Friday.

Charlie is shown standing beside a woman in a long shawl a short distance away and pointing to the right. There's a thought bubble showing him thinking about his father, two sisters and his dog back home at Ogoki Post.

The woman, supposedly Charles Kelly's wife Clara, is shown handing Charlie a jar of wooden matches. She then puts her right hand affectionately on his shoulder as the man and two boys look on outside the cabin door.

There's a thought bubble showing her imagining Charlie warming himself alone by a fire out in the bush. As Charlie walks off with a smile on his face, one of the boys waves goodbye.

Gord Downie's lyrics say:

> She gave me matches
> Seven wooden matches
> She put them into a small slim glass jar
> With a screwtop lid
> I fingered that jar
> I put it in my pocket
> She said, "Can't go into the woods without them."
> I smiled at her and left

This segment in *Secret Path* is completely at odds with the article in *Maclean's* magazine, the reports in the *Kenora Daily Miner and News,* what Principal Colin Wasacase wrote at the time and, also, what he told me when I interviewed him in Kenora.

And, again, how could any responsible adult turn a 12-year-old loose like that with no idea of where he's going?

There's no trace anywhere in *Secret Path* of the day and a night Charlie spent at the cabin on Charles Kelly's trapline at Mud Lake. Neither is there anything showing Mr. Kelly turning him loose at the railway tracks with no food or water.

\* \* \*

In a statement he released on September 9, 2016, after meeting with Charlie's family at Ogoki Post, Gord Downie said his brother Mike had given him a copy of Ian Adams' February, 1967, article in *Maclean's* magazine.

Best-selling author Joseph Boyden, whose book *Wenjack* is also used in the schools, was quoted in the *Globe and Mail* on October 19, 2016 saying: "Mike Downie, Gord Downie's brother, had brought to our attention an old *Maclean's* article, from 1967. Mike gave me the article and I was fascinated by it."

It's clear from the above that Gord Downie and his brother Mike had read Ian Adam's article in *Maclean's* describing Charlie's overnight stay at Mr. Kelly's trapline cabin.

And yet, there is no mention of it in *Secret Path*. Instead, school children reading the book are left with a picture of a warm, caring, Clara Kelly giving him a jar of wooden matches just before he heads off into the bush with a happy smile on his face.

Surely even the authors of *Secret Path* would have known that that was a totally irresponsible thing to do to a child. Talk about abuse!

The Downie brothers drew cartoonist Jeff Lemire's attention to a 10-song album about Charlie that Gord Downie was recording in the winter of 2014.

Mr. Lemire was asked to create the drawings for *Secret Path* which was to be released at the same time as the album in October, 2016, to mark the 50th anniversary of Charlie's death.

An animated film, *The Secret Path*, based on Gord Downie's music and Jeff Lemire's drawings, was broadcast as an hour-long commercial-free television special on the CBC on Sunday, October 23, 2016.

* * *

Later on in *Secret Path*, there's a drawing showing a shivering Charlie sitting alone on the railway tracks beside a small fire. Gord Downie's lyrics on the opposite page say: "Run along the river. On the Secret Path. I will not be struck. I'm not going back."

There is no evidence that Charlie was physically abused at any time during the three years he was at Cecilia Jeffrey Indian Residential School.

Further on in the book, Mr. Downie's lyrics say:

> And the fuck-off rocks
> Along the tracks
> Secret Path
> There's no "Secret Path"

You can't say fuck in the newspapers or on radio or TV. And yet here it is in a book that's being read by elementary students in more than 65,000 classrooms across Canada and in the United States.

In what would appear to be a backhanded slap at the dedicated staff at Cecilia Jeffrey Indian Residential School, Gord Downie has Charlie say:

> I've seen how they are
> How they'd all sell their souls
> In little bits and pieces till they get old
> You don't make a dent
> In indifference
> Ya gotta haunt them, haunt them, haunt them

That's most certainly not the way the staff were described in the more than 300 positive letters students and parents wrote at, or around, the three years Charlie was at Cecilia Jeffrey Indian Residential School.

Towards the end of *Secret Path*, there's a drawing showing Charlie stumbling along snow-covered railway tracks in a failed attempt to reach his home at the remote fly-in community of Ogoki Post, about 600 kilometres northeast of Kenora.

A long, bony hand with open fingers stretches out across the sky above Charlie. And then, he's shown looking warily at an imaginary male in clerical collar with a white cross on his chest looking menacingly at him from among the trees.

One of the last drawings in *Secret Path* shows Charlie, curled up and shivering from the cold, dying beside the railway tracks.

It's a very poignant and compelling story. But it's more fiction than fact.

\* \* \*

It is clear from comments students have made after reading *Secret Path* that they believe it is a true account of Charlie's last six days.

They have no way of knowing that it is a complete fabrication and bears no resemblance to the positive experiences described in the more than 300 letters written by students and parents over the six years prior to Charlie's death on October 22, 1966.

An example of the impact reading *Secret Path* has had on young minds can be found in a Grade 5 student at Toronto's Dundas Junior Public School who said the drawings made him feel "mad and sad."

One of his classmates said Charlie's story "has impacted our lives and we want change…if we can continue to educate kids around the world history will not repeat itself."

Charlie's story needs to be told, another student said "because it's just not him that went through these troubles."

Another student said "it is not only ourselves that matter because we shouldn't be treating people a different way because of the way they look and the way they are."

Those impressionable, compassionate, young minds had no way of knowing that most of the information in *Secret Path* has no basis in fact. And their parents had no idea of the extent to which their children were being misinformed.

One of the Grade 6 students at Pilot Butte School, about 20 kilometres northeast of Regina, Saskatchewan, copied the drawing in *Secret Path* of a priest approaching Charlie's bed. In a thought bubble she drew above the boy's head, she wrote Gord Downie's lyric: "Don't let this touch you."

There is no credible evidence that Charlie Wenjack was physically or sexually abused at any time during the three years he was at Cecilia Jeffrey Indian Residential School.

\* \* \*

As the 1997 article in *Maclean's* seemed to be the source of information for *Secret Path*, I did a search to see what it actually said. I read the article very carefully to determine to what extent it could have been the source for some of the most disturbing images and lyrics in *Secret Path*.

The first thing I noticed was that the article clearly stated that Cecilia Jeffrey Indian Residential School was operated by the Protestant Presbyterian Church in Canada. Contrary to the drawings in *Secret Path*, there was no mention of there being any nuns or priests at the school.

Not a single word in the article supported the drawings showing nuns delousing naked Ojibway boys, the priest dragging a screaming girl by the arm, the nun yanking on the boy's ear until he yelled in pain, or the pedophile priest approaching Charlie.

There wasn't anything to support Gord Downie's lyrics about Charlie refusing to "be struck again" or of a molested Charlie saying "don't let this touch you."

*Why would they make that stuff up? What possible motive could there be for doing something like that? None of that is in the Maclean's article.*

It would appear that the way Cecilia Jeffrey Indian Residential School is misrepresented in *Secret Path* is because that's the way Charlie's sisters described it to the Downie brothers.

As Mike Downie said while being interviewed by author Tanya Talaga in October 2019, neither one of them knew very much at all about Canada's Indian residential schools.

"I was driving in my car and heard this [CBC radio] story of this little boy running away from his residential school," Mr. Downie said. "And my first reaction was, 'Residential school,' and 'Wonder what that is?' And I just knew nothing about it, about Indian Residential Schools."

The podcast was produced by the Gord Downie & Chanie Wenjack Fund in advance of a Secret Path Live concert that was to be held at Toronto's Roy Thompson Hall on October 19, 2019.

"And I went home, I looked up, there was lots more information about Chanie Wenjack, in particular, and including the article by Ian Adams from *Maclean's* in 1967, 'The Lonely Death of Charlie Wenjack'," Mr. Downie continued. "And I printed that up, and Gord and I were having lunch the next day, and we sat down and I pushed the article across to him, and I said, 'You just can't believe this story.' And that's kinda where it all started."

Given their almost total lack of knowledge about the Indian residential schools, the Downie brothers would have had no reason not to take Charlie's sisters at their word about the circumstances of Charlie's death.

Back on June 17, 2010, one of Charlie's sisters was at a Truth and Reconciliation Commission event in Winnipeg.

During a women's sharing circle, someone whose name was not recorded, said:

> "My brother Charlie [Wenjack]...he died running away from school. He was only twelve. After being hit by a principal, after being sexually abused, sodomized by another older student. I wanted him to have been here, to say that all he wanted was to go home. That's all he wanted. He didn't want anything else. But it took two days to get here...And that's a long ways. He tried to walk that. In 1966, October 22, he froze to death trying to walk home....
>
> "And whatever money I get from my IAP [Independent Assessment Process for former students who suffered abuse.], I want to get a healing centre for my reserve, with Charlie's name."

In fact, we can go back even farther than that. Back to **24** years before the Wenjack and Downie families first became acquainted.

Indigenous author Lee Maracle wrote about Charlie in her 1990 *Sojourner's Truth and Other Stories*.

Like *Secret Path*, Ms. Maracle changed Presbyterian Cecilia Jeffrey Indian Residential School into a Catholic institution.

She wrote that Charlie's shyness was not unusual for Indigenous children. "His silence was interpreted by the priests and the catholic lay teachers as stoic reserve—a quality inherited from his pagan ancestors. It was regarded in the same way the religious viewed the children's tearless response to punishment: a quaint combination of primitive courage and lack of emotion. All the children were like this and so Charlie could not be otherwise."

That's not what the students and parents said in the more than 300 positive letters they wrote during the eight years before Charlie's death.

Ms. Maracle's *Sojourner's Truth and Other Stories* described Cecilia Jeffrey Indian Residential School as a virtual horror chamber. "The thrashing he [Charlie] knew could be counted on for committing the crime of daydreaming was not worth the reward," she wrote.

In her version of what happened that sunny afternoon in October, 1966: "He [Charlie] rushed breathless to the closet and grabbed a jacket. The other boys had already tied the rope to the metal latticing that closed the windows. Each boy squeezed through the square created by one missing strip of metal lattice, and, hanging on to the rope, swung out from the window, then dropped to the ground below."

This is a complete distortion of what actually happened. Charlie and the McDonald brothers were on the swings in the playground.

Ms. Maracle continues: "Safe in the bosom of the forest, after a tense but joyous run across the yard, the boys let go the cramped spirit that the priesthood so painstakingly tried to destroy in them. They whooped, they hollered, bayed at the moon [it was afternoon] and romped about chucking snow [There was no snow that day.] in loose, small balls at each other."

The events Ms. Maracle described in *Sojourner's Truth and Other Stories* most definitely did not happen.

In an email I sent to her on December 4, 2017, I said I simply didn't understand why people felt it was okay to take Charlie's story and turn it into a pretzel of misinformation.

"What is the purpose behind it all," I asked. "Why doesn't Charlie have the right to his own story?"

In an email that she sent in reply, Ms. Maracle said she got much of her information from Charlie's family and now realized that most of it was incorrect.

"We did not twist his life so much as have had his life twisted for us," she wrote. "I empathize with the family members **in their misinforming us** [emphasis added]."

She said she had reread the book and realized the extent to which she got things wrong. "It is horrifying to me now," she wrote, "but I understand because of how we [Indigenous people] were then [back in 1990 when her book was published]."

A CBC report on September 5, 2012,—two years before hooking up with the Downie brothers—said Charlie's older sister Pearl

Achneepineskum said she believed that he was "sexually assaulted, prompting him to run away from the school and die of exposure. Achneepineskum and others are asking for a new, more thorough investigation into Charlie's death."

In an interview with *Globe and Mail* columnist Denise Balkissoon published on October 18, 2016, author Joseph Boyden said: "This beautiful little 12-year-old, shy boy, he ran away from school, **his family tells me** [emphasis added], because he was being sexually abused. It's disgusting."

There would appear to be no doubt that Charlie's older sisters truly believed he was sexually abused and passed their concerns on to the Downie brothers, Joseph Boyden and others.

However, even if that was true, we have already established that Charlie had no intention of running away on the sunny afternoon of Sunday, October 16, 1966.

The McDonald brothers had decided that it was a good day to visit their uncle at his cabin and Charlie tagged along with them.

If they had decided to explore downtown Kenora instead and return to the school in time for dinner, he would most likely have gone along with that also.

\* \* \*

Despite the fact most of what is said and shown in *Secret Path* has no basis in fact, the government of Prime Minister Justin Trudeau gave the Gord Downie and Chanie (Charlie) Wenjack Fund $5 million in 2018 to, among other things, promote *Secret Path*.

According to the government's budget document, the purpose of the Gord Downie & Chanie Wenjack Fund was "to continue the conversation that began with Chanie [Charlie] Wenjack's residential **school story** [emphasis added]."

Nothing in the budget document said what criteria the government used in awarding $5 million to the Fund. Nor was there anything about how the Fund—which was less than two years old and didn't even have charitable status at the time—would be required to account for the money.

According to the Fund's website, it didn't receive official status as a charitable organization until **after** the $5 million was announced.

A statement on its website later said: "In March of 2018, the Gord Downie & Chanie Wenjack Fund (DWF) received its official status as a charitable organization. (Prior to this we operated as a project of Tides Canada.)."

Tides Canada posted an item on its website on July 11, 2017, that said: "Meet the Downie Wenjack Fund one of our newest projects on the shared platform. Mike and Gord Downie, alongside the Wenjack family, launched the Fund to continue the conversation that began with Chanie Wenjack's residential school story."

Tides Canada is an American-financed, anti-Canadian oil sands organization that has poured millions into the fight against Canadian pipeline projects—including the Trans Mountain pipeline which the federal government purchased from Kinder Morgan for $4.5 billion in August, 2018.

In an article published in the *Financial Post* on March 21, 2018, former BC Attorney General/Justice Minister Suzanne Anton said: "The U.S.-based Tides Foundation, for example, directs funds to Canadian organizations such as Dogwood Initiative and Leadnow, both of whom featured prominently in the anti-pipeline protest on March 10th in Burnaby, and both of whom take an active role in B.C. elections, aiming to get pro-energy politicians out of office and anti-pipeline politicians elected….

"Over the last few years Tides has granted $40 million to 100 Canadian anti-pipeline organizations who, in return, have done a fine job of constraining the Canadian economy and saving money for American buyers of Canadian oil."

Part of the Trudeau government's $5 million was to be used to enable the Fund to partner "with educators and Indigenous communities to develop curricula for Canadian schools that **accurately** [Emphasis added] describe Indigenous history."

There was no mention of what, if any, relevant experience those employed by the Fund possessed that would qualify them to "develop curricula for Canadian schools."

# Chapter 16

**CHARLIE'S OLDER SISTERS** Pearl Achneepineskum and Daisy Munroe visit schools across Canada and, by their presence, put the stamp of approval on what *Secret Path* says about their little brother's death.

According to the Gord Downie & Chanie Wenjack Fund: "Pearl and Daisy have been advocates for sharing Chanie's [Charlie's] story. They have been seen at WE Days across Canada, and on the Secret Path Live tour in 2016. Their goal is to share Chanie's story with all who will listen and to prevent such atrocities from taking place again."

A video of the sisters' visit to the Grade 5 class at Toronto's Dundas Junior Public School was produced by Gord and Mike Downie. It was made available for downloading on the CBC Short Docs platform in June, 2017.

The onscreen introduction to the video titled *The Secret Path: In The Classroom* said *Secret Path* "tells **the true story** (emphasis added) of Chanie Wenjack, a 12 year old boy who **escaped** (emphasis added) a residential school and tried to walk 600 kilometres home."

The teacher had made *Secret Path* part of the curriculum and the students read it prior to the visit and had been asked to draw pictures about Charlie's experience and write letters to his family.

Most of the film was shot in the classroom and there were clips of Ms. Achneepineskum talking at a picnic table outside the school.

While sitting at the picnic table, she said she had felt that the disturbing pictures in *Secret Path* might be too graphic for the students.

"The *Secret Path* is so graphic," she said, "that I thought children would not be able to handle it. I was hesitant in introducing it to the children. I just thought they wouldn't handle it. It couldn't register to them. There was just too much pain for them."

Ms. Achneepineskum also said: "They [Grade 5 students] were amazed with what we went through because they haven't and they can't fathom what pain we went through."

That comment would have come as somewhat of a surprise to the students who were at Cecilia Jeffrey at the same time as Ms. Achneepineskum and called the principal and his wife "Mom" and "Dad", signed their letters "Love" and thanked them for being such good parents to them.

In October, 2016, Ms. Achneepineskum said on Global News: "Even though the pictures [in *Secret Path*] are very graphic, they do tell the truth. Whoever did this got the real picture of what happened."

CBC broadcast an interview on October 20, 2016, in which Ms. Achneepineskum said: "The story of Charlie [sic] should have never happened. The death that he went through and the pictures that were done [in *Secret Path*] were very graphic but it was the stark truth."

She knew, from having attended Cecilia Jeffrey, that that there were no nuns or priests there. She also knew that her brother was attending a nearby public school.

And she also knew that there is no evidence to support the drawings of nuns delousing naked Ojibway boys, the priest dragging a screaming girl by the arm, the nun yanking on the boy's ear until he yelled in pain, or the pedophile priest molesting Charlie.

You might recall that the children had been asked to make drawings expressing their feelings about Charlie. One little girl used colors that reminded her of him. Blue to represent sadness, red to represent flatness and black to represent "the darkness of like dying."

In talking about the picture when she was at the picnic table outside the school, Ms. Achneepineskum said: "When she said that to me and described the picture, yeah, that's exactly the feelings that the residential school children felt."

Not only did Ms. Achneepineskum vouch for the accuracy of the drawings and lyrics in *Secret Path*, she painted an even grimmer picture when she was with the Grade 5 students.

"Some of the kids when we went to school just disappeared," she told the attentive children. "It's only now that we found out that there's actually graveyards across where we were going to school.

"The tie that binds us when we're in a residential school that's the only love and affection we knew was from another child so it was very precious to us when one of our friends disappeared."

Later, at the picnic table, she said: "The graveyard, that was reality. It wasn't just a story. That's real life."

A document published by the National Centre for Truth and Reconciliation showed no deaths during the 11 years Ms. Achneepineskum attended the school.

As for the graveyard she told the students about, former staffer Abe Loewen believed she was most likely referring to the Ojibwa Presbyterian Cemetery at the other end of Round Lake.

The Grade 5 students had no way of knowing that Ms. Achneepineskum's claim that some of her fellow students "just disappeared" had no basis in fact.

At the end of the video, the children are shown participating in a traditional smudging ceremony and they all hold hands in a circle along with the teachers and Charlie's sisters. Ms. Achneepineskum sings a traditional Ojibway prayer.

The teacher is then shown saying: "I just want my students to be able to take this with them throughout their lives and to know that one little thing can make a huge difference. And it doesn't matter how old or young they are they can do really good things in this world and bring about change and hope. I couldn't be more proud of them."

I wonder how she would have reacted if she had been told that most of what her students were being taught about Charlie Wenjack and Cecilia Jeffrey Indian Residential School was patently untrue.

\* \* \*

According to a September 5, 2012, report on the CBC, Ms. Achneepineskum, claimed that students at Cecilia Jeffrey were often dressed in special clothes and told to smile for photos.

"Achneepineskum says the photos never captured the abuse many children suffered there," the report said. "She believes 12-year-old Charlie was sexually assaulted, prompting him to run away from the school and die of exposure. Achneepineskum and others are asking for a new, more thorough investigation into Charlie's death."

Despite the claims made by Ms. Achneepineskum and in *Secret Path*, there is no evidence that Charlie was sexually assaulted at Cecilia Jeffrey. And, as you will recall, he did not run away or "escape."

While attending the renaming of a Thunder Bay Indigenous training institute in memory of her brother in January, 2018, Pearl Achneepineskum said the children who attended Cecilia Jeffrey Indian Residential School continued to struggle with lasting, generational impacts.

"It's part of us," tbnewswatch.com quoted her as saying. "When you are taken at six years old, it's something you have to contend with. You grow up fast. At six years old you have to fend for yourself. Everything you went through at that school, it stayed with you. It has stayed with me. I also see others who have gone to school and I see those same traits that I see in myself."

Ms. Achneepineskum said she was very proud to see her brother's name associated with an organization that was bringing education and training to Indigenous youth across the region.

"The institution that we went to, I suppose was meant to be a good opportunity for us, but they neglected to consider the feelings of the children," she said. "My brother just wouldn't accept that and that is why he ran away. Otherwise, if it [he] had been at home, it would have been a different story."

In a report on CBC news the next day, Ms. Achneepineskum said" "All he [Charlie] wanted to do was to go home, to run away from the environment he was forced into....When I was there, at the school, I could not learn, I was too busy being lonely. Loneliness, now, is part of my life. It has stayed with me because I had to accept it when I was six years old."

\*\*\*

Canadian author Joseph Boyden wrote the script for a widely-publicized Heritage Minute about Charlie's death which was released on National Indigenous Day, June 21, 2016.

The one-minute video was produced by Historica Canada and financed by the government of Ontario.

It was narrated by Charlie's sister Pearl Achneepineskum and Joseph Boyden.

The video opens with a gasping Charlie running out of the back door of a school looking anxiously over his shoulder as if someone is chasing him and heading for the bush.

That scene conflicts with an October, 2016 article in *Maclean's* magazine in which Mr. Boyden is quoted as saying: "None of them had planned to escape on that unseasonably warm autumn afternoon."

Ms. Achneepineskum's voice is heard saying: "Charlie [the caption changed it to Chanie] wanted to go back home. It was a thousand kilometres away."

As you will recall from the article in *Maclean's* and the reports in the *Kenora Daily Miner and News,* Charlie's home was about 600 kilometres away, not 1,000.

"More than 150,000 of us children had to go," Ms. Achneepinsekum says.

As Charlie is shown running through the bush, Ms. Achneepineskum says: "They forced him to go to the Indian residential school."

Someone is shown cutting Charlie's hair. "They wanted to change us," Ms. Achneepineskum says.

Ojibway boys in pyjamas are shown holding their hands in prayer at the foot of the mattresses on their bunk beds.

A priest in clerical collar barks: "Our father in heaven."

"Our father in heaven," the boys respond in unison.

"Hallowed be your name," the priest says.

"Hallowed be your name," the boys respond.

Priest: "Thy kingdom come."

Boys: "Thy kingdom come."

Priest: "Thy will be done."

Boys: "Thy will be done."

At that point Ms. Achneepineskum says: "Kill the Indian in the child."

Again, there were no priests at Cecilia Jeffrey Indian Residential School. It was operated by the Women's Missionary Society of the Presbyterian Church in Canada. None of the staff wore clerical garb.

And, given the positive letters from parents and students and the fact that the students were allowed to speak their native language outside of class or in the presence of staff, there was no effort to "kill the Indian in the child."

The priest notices that Charlie isn't praying with the others, grabs him by the arm and throws him onto a bed in another room.

Ms. Achneepineskum: "It's been called cultural genocide."

We then see a family photo of a smiling Charlie.

Ms. Achneepineskum: "I survived the residential schools. My brother Chanie didn't."

Charlie's dead body is shown lying beside the railway tracks.

The Historica Canada caption says: "A part of our heritage."

As the camera pulls back to show Charlie's dead body farther and farther away, Joseph Boyden intones: "Chanie Wenjack was one of thousands of children who died in Canada's Indian residential school system. More than 80,000 survivors and their families still live with this legacy today."

A CBC News report about the Heritage Minute said: "Making its premiere on National Indigenous Day, Historica Canada's newest Heritage Minute explores the dark history of Indian residential schools and their lasting effects on Indigenous people."

"This is something we need to talk about," Joseph Boyden said, "and we need to recognize as Canadians, that our history is not always good."

The CBC report mistakenly said: "Wenjack's death prompted the first inquest into the treatment of children at the schools."

In fact there had been several inquests into the deaths of children who had attended the schools. As far back as 1902, for example, an inquest was held into the death of an eight-year-old boy whose father found him dead from exposure after running away from Williams Lake Indian Industrial School which was located between Kamloops and Prince George, British Columbia.

In 1937, an inquest was held into the deaths of four boys who froze to death after running away from the Lejac Residential School west of Prince George, British Columbia'

Charlie's inquest was most definitely not the first.

"He's [Charlie] a powerful symbol of those innocents who ran, just trying to be home, and didn't make it, who didn't survive residential school," Mr. Boyden said

In a video Historica Canada provided to the media, Ms. Achneepineskum said: "My brother, when he died, he didn't take life for granted. He knew where he was wanting to be. His whole happiness was home.

"When other people see this film, I hope they take away that they're very fortunate that they can do whatever they like and not being stopped of being who they are; that they're proud of who they are."

The CBC report said Mr. Boyden believed it was important that the Heritage Minutes should be told from the perspective of Indigenous people.

"We've all seen the Heritage Minutes," he said, "and they're great, but it's always from the side of the settler."

Anthony Wilson-Smith, the president and chief executive officer of Historica Canada, said: "I always say that if all people know of Canadian history or a particular issue is what they've learned from one of our minutes, that's not nearly enough.

"What we hope to do is get people to watch a minute and say, 'I never knew that ... and I really want to know more about that.'"

The problem with "I never knew **that**" is that, like Gord Downie's *Secret Path*, the Heritage Minute about Charlie Wenjack is a total fabrication.

On its website, Historica Canada says: "In all our programs, **we place a premium on accuracy** [emphasis added] and context, and work with subject matter experts toward those ends."

On November 23, 2017, the *Waterloo Record* published an opinion piece critical of the Heritage Minute, Gord Downie's *Secret Path* and Joseph Boyden's *Wenkack* which was written by *Maclean's* editor-at-large Peter Shawn-Taylor

"So," Mr. Shawn-Taylor asked, "why is the story of Chanie [Charlie] Wenjack so full of imaginative fabrication?"

Mr. Shawn-Taylor found it totally unacceptable that the Heritage Minute and *Secret Path* had transformed a Protestant Indian residential school into a Catholic horror chamber.

He also said: "Writer Robert MacBain can take credit for being the first to reveal the invention of Chanie's sexual abuse in the online publication C2C Journal [October 2, 2017]. He's also the author of 'Their Home and Native Land', a careful and sympathetic look at native relations in Canada, and was for many years a consultant with the Department of Indian Affairs, often travelling to Kenora and visiting Cecilia Jeffrey school while in operation."

Mr. Shawn-Taylor quoted me as saying: "Downie and others have built up this child into a symbol of all the horrors that happened with the residential school system. But he is a real person who is entitled to his own story."

In response to Mr. Shawn-Taylor's criticism of the Heritage Minute about Charlie, Anthony Wilson-Smith wrote a letter to the editor of the *Waterloo Record* in which he said: "The Minute depicts Chanie being shoved into an isolation room as punishment for misbehaviour. That was a well-documented form of discipline at residential schools, and that is the extent of punishment portrayed."

There is no evidence, anywhere, of Charlie ever having been shoved into an isolation room.

In response to the criticism about having a Catholic priest in charge of Ojibway boys at a Protestant school, Mr. Wilson Smith said the Heritage Minute does not "make any reference to the Roman Catholic Church—because we knew from our research that this school was Presbyterian in religious denomination."

Given that they knew the school was Protestant, that begs the question of why Historica Canada considered it appropriate to change Cecilia Jeffrey to a Catholic school.

Mr. Wilson-Smith concluded his letter by stating emphatically that "it is undeniable that Chanie's wrenching experiences at his residential school prompted the circumstances, as briefly revisited in our Minute, that led to his death."

There is no evidence of any "wrenching experiences" that prompted a lonely Charlie Wenjack to tag along with the McDonald brothers on their trip to their uncle's cabin.

In fact, if it had been raining that afternoon, he might very well have been alive today.

Historica Canada has prepared an "education guide" about Charlie to be used in schools across Canada.

"As a class, watch the 'Chanie Wenjack' Heritage Minute," the guide says. "After, respond to the following questions together in groups. Read more about Chanie at *The Canadian Encylopedia* [Which is published by Historica Canada].

"A. Why do you think Chanie chose to run away from residential school? What does this say about conditions students faced in the school?

"B. The quote in the Minute, 'Kill the Indian in the child', was frequently used to describe the aim of the residential schools. What does this tell you about the intentions of the policies that led to the formation of the Indian residential school system in Canada? Do you think the quote accurately reflects the intentions of the residential schools?"

The education guide also says: "According to his family, Chanie Wenjack's name was changed to 'Charlie' by the people who ran the Cecilia Jeffrey Indian Residential School. What does this tell you about cultural repression and assimilation? How does this contribute to feelings of disconnection and alienation? What do you think were the goals and impacts of name changing?"

\* \* \*

During Secret Path Week in October, 2019, students from across Canada and all the way down to Hoover, Alabama, tuned in to a live podcast featuring Charlie's sisters, Pearl Achneepineskum and Daisy Munroe.

The sisters were surrounded by Indigenous students in a classroom at Dennis Franklin Cromarty High School in Thunder Bay, Ontario, which provides schooling for Indigenous students from far-away reserves who board in the city.

The host was Joe Grabowski, the founder and Executive Director of Exploring by the Seat of Your Pants.

In opening the podcast, Mr. Grabowski said the goal of the Gord Downie & Chanjie Wenjack Fund "is to continue the conversation that began with Chanie Wenjack's **residential school story** [emphasis added] and to support the reconciliation process through awareness, education, and action."

He also said: "Pearl and Daisy have been incredible advocates for sharing their brother's story, especially with Canada's youth. We've got a great group of classrooms from across North America, tuning in with us, and we're looking forward to hearing your brother's story from your perspective."

Pearl Achneepineskum said: "The reason why the story was told, I was the one that was at home when they brought **Charlie** [emphasis added] home in a coffin. That turned my life around, and almost hit rock bottom.

"But I thought that this wasn't going to end at that time. I had always wanted to tell his story. And so, that's what I began to do. Whoever'd listen, I would tell them what…what had happened. And the impact, the impacts that I saw from that.

"It wasn't just only me. It was my whole family, and it was especially my parents. My parents had hit rock bottom with his death. They never understood and the government uh, promised us that they would take care of him.

"And when that happened, when I saw my parents um, not almost recover from that, that's when I went really (inaudible) to try and tell his story.

"And it came about, that was back in 1966. And I kept on going. And every meeting that I went, I would tell anybody the story.

If I met people on the plane, I would tell, especially the white people, the story.

"I wanted to make everybody aware of what happened with these little kids. These little kids that were promised a golden future. Safety. And love. Those actually were the ones that were absent in our life. The promises that was made to those, to the children.

"They're absent, they were absent in life because no one at that school really thought of them as human beings.

"And I had also wanted to have the children heard, rather than uh, being told to be quiet. I wanted children's voices to be laughing. I wanted children to be seen. And if that, if that is what it takes to expose these children to be thought of as human beings, then so be it.

"I know when I walk this road again, over and over again, I know it hurts. But I want to do that. There's many tears that fall when I walk this road again. But to save the lives of the little children that only want to live, that only want to enjoy life, I'll do it.

Her sister, Daisy Munroe, joined in: "It was no such thing as cell phones at that time. There was a…there was a phone, but it was a one ring, two kinda phone. And you happened to be at that booth, you could pick up a phone. Uh, there always was no, any way to communicate to back home, kinda thing, 'cause the only way I found out about his death was CBC. CBC aired it from Winnipeg. And uh, when that happened, they just uh, started shipping us home."

NOTE: School officials informed Ms. Munroe about her brother's death the day after his lifeless body was found lying beside the railway tracks. His name wasn't released until three days after his body was found.

"The way we found out," Ms. Achneepineskum told the students, "was that the day that they brought our, his coffin home. That was the time that we found out that he had, you know, passed on. Nothing was said before."

NOTE: School officials notified Charlie's mother the day after his body was found. Meanwhile, the OPP were trying to contact his father by radio phone.

# Chapter 17

A REPORT THAT was published in *The Signal* on November 21, 2016, said that *Secret Path* was going to be part of the curriculum for schools in Nova Scotia starting in September, 2017.

Wyatt White, director of Mi'kmaq services for the Nova Scotia Department of Education and Early Childhood Development was quoted saying: "*Secret Path* has come along and really been the wedge that opened the door to learning this [Indian residential school] history in a new way."

The report in the *Signal* said *Secret Path* "tells the story of Chanie Wenjack, who was only 12 years old when he died after escaping from his Ontario residential school in 1966. He was trying to walk 400 miles back home."

It also said that Mr. White, who was overseeing the introduction of *Secret Path* to classrooms across Nova Scotia, "was one of 33 educators from across the country who attended an October meeting in Ottawa to discuss how *Secret Path* can be used in schools. The Wenjack family, Gord Downie's brother Mike, and Jeff Lemire were also at the meeting."

The report quoted Mr. White saying: "This story is a gateway for students to learn about the residential school history in their own area, not just the one told in the story. *Secret Path* has created an opportunity for educators across the country to find out who the Chanie Wenjacks are in our own provinces."

Some teachers in Nova Scotia had already started using *Secret Path* in their classrooms. Others were expected to receive professional development materials related to the project before the next September.

"We're sensitive to the fact that this is not a simple or easy area for teachers to take on, especially if they're not as familiar with the subject matter," Mr. White said. "We want to make sure they have enough support to be able to use it in their classrooms well."

According to the report in *The* Signal, students across Nova Scotia would start studying Secret Path in full in Grade 7. It was also believed that certain parts of the project would be used at the elementary level as a means of introducing younger students to the subject.

"We're working to determine the foundation kids need to have in place about the Mi'kmaq community and Indigenous people in Canada, so when the topic of residential schools comes up, they're emotionally ready to learn about it," Mr. White said.

Spencer Wilmot, director of education with the Native Council of Nova Scotia, was quoted as saying: "I think the sooner students understand what Aboriginal people went through with the residential school system, the better. Our own Aboriginal students need to know their past as well."

\* \* \*

On April 26, 2017, The Manitoba Teachers' Society announced that it had prepared lesson plans based on *Secret Path* to be used in classrooms across Manitoba.

The press release said *Secret Path* "chronicles the story of Chanie Wenjack, a 12-year-old boy who died after running away from Residential school in the 1960s."

According to the press release, a group of Indigenous and non-Indigenous teachers from across Manitoba had been assembled to "discuss and explore the *Secret Path* and to create lesson and unit plans to support the use of this resource for the teaching about Residential schools in Manitoba classrooms.

"The culmination of the discussions and work of this tremendous group of teachers is found here. We want to hear from other teachers who are willing to share lessons or unit plans."

In the lesson plans, students in Grades 1 to 3 were asked to compare and contrast their classroom with what was purported to be Charlie's classroom in *Secret Path*.

As I pointed out earlier, Charlie didn't attend class at Cecilia Jeffrey. He was attending a nearby public school at the time of his death and only boarded there.

The students were asked to note that there were "no books or toys" in the classroom.

Toys? The lad was 12 years old. Even if that **was** his classroom, there wouldn't be any toys there.

The students were asked to discuss "the expressions on the children's faces" and "use different words to describe emotions/feelings."

Each and every child in *Secret Path's* fabricated classroom has an expressionless look on its face.

There isn't a scrap of paper or anything else on their desks.

Their arms are hanging lifeless at their sides.

Their eyes are shut tight as if waiting for someone to whack them with a big stick.

The students were asked to note that the pictures of the school were drawn in black and white and Charlie's thought bubbles about his far-away family and home were in colour.

And then, to top it all off, the students were asked to "write a note of encouragement to Chanie or to another Residential school survivor."

How many parents in Manitoba would have known that what their children were being taught is patently untrue?

\* \* \*

On November 17, 2017, Peterborough radio station CHEX broadcast a report about local teacher Mitch Champagne who had developed lesson plans based on *Secret Path*.

"I saw this as an opportunity to keep working with Gord's work, because the students really responded to it," Mr. Champagne said.

Reporter Dan Nyznik said: "When Champagne was going to schools, he never learned much about Canadian history, especially what happened at residential schools, so he created lessons for his Grades 7 and 8 students, focusing on Chanie Wenjack."

"He's [Charlie] one of you know, 100,000, 150,000 students that attended residential schools," Mr. Champagne said, "but the fact that he's 12 years old, and I'm sitting in a room with 12-year-olds, these kids hear this story and they, they feel genuine emotion."

The report then plays clips from students.

"It's really too bad that he couldn't see his mom or dad at my age, and that shouldn't be happening at that time" one student said.

"I like learning about how he couldn't speak English," another said, "so he had to figure out his own ways to learn how to communicate with the other people.

Reporter Nyznik then says: "Most of the students say they like learning about this chapter in our history, despite its dark tone. Champagne believes the teachings go beyond the classroom."

At that point Mr. Champagne says: "Because of Gord's popularity, you know, the kids are going home and telling their parents what they're learning, and then, the parents are having these discussions about you know, reconciliation, at their tables, which is, I couldn't for a, a better outcome than that."

That is followed by a short clip of Gord Downie singing one of the songs from the *Secret Path* album.

In finishing the report, Mr. Nyznik says: "Champagne's lessons can be found on the Trent University website, where he also teaches."

\* \* \*

Students at Thunder Bay's Pope John Paul II School paid tribute to students who had attended Indian residential schools on November 20, 2017.

According to a report in *Thunder Bay News Watch*: "Students were also introduced to *The Stranger*, a video created as part of former Tragically Hip front-man Gord Downie's *The Secret Path* project, detailing the life and death of 12-year-old Chanie Wenjack, who died trying to escape a residential school in Kenora in the late 1960s, attempting to walk more than 600 kilometres to Ogoki Post.

Principal Don Grant was quoted as saying *Secret Path* showed students "the harsh realities that existed. For some of our younger students, who weren't aware of those unfortunate scenarios, it's important to be able to get the facts straight, as our own government has through truth and reconciliation, decided to move forward through positive ways as we can, but to understand what has happened in the past."

One of my colleagues in Thunder Bay sent Trustee Philip Pelletier a copy of Peter Shawn-Taylor's op-ed in the *Waterloo Record* exposing *Secret Path* as a complete distortion of the Charlie Wenjack story.

Trustee Pelletier forwarded my colleague's email with the op-ed from the *Waterloo Record* to Superintendent Omer Belisle of the Thunder Bay Catholic District School Board.

Despite the fact the authors of *Secret Path* had transformed a Protestant school into a Catholic horror chamber, Superintendent Belisle replied: "The truth is being taught in recent curriculum changes grades 4-10 to start then K-12 on its way soon- all taught with age appropriate strategies

"This story has brought light in a national way-we embrace it. Feel free to pass on my contact Info."

*\* \* \**

A ceremony was held on October 17, 2018, to celebrate a partnership between the Gord Downie & Chanie Wenjack Fund and the North Vancouver School District.

Under the partnership agreement, *Secret Path* was going to be used in the classrooms to teach students about the Indian residential school system.

District Principal Brad Baker, one of the primary movers of the new partnership, was quoted as saying: "It's so heart-wrenching that a young boy was ripped away from his family and endured abuses at the school just for wanting to go back home."

The ceremony was held at the site of the former St. Paul's Indian Residential School in central Vancouver. A report in *North Shore News* said the ceremony was the "kick-off of the first annual Secret Path week."

The report also said: "Wenjack died in 1966, and 50 years later his story has become the centrepiece of a new campaign to inform all Canadians about the horrors of the government-sponsored residential school system—a system that was created to erase the history and culture of First Nations people and assimilate them into Euro-Canadian culture—and to work towards reconciliation."

One year later, Mr. Baker was interviewed by author Tanya Talaga in a podcast produced by the Gord Downie & Chanie Wenjack Fund.

"I'm the son of an Indian residential school survivor," Mr. Baker said, "and when Gord first brought Chanie's story to light after the Secret Path, I thought it was important to continue that work and bringing Chanie's story to students in my school district, and also for those students to bring it home to their parents."

Mr. Baker went on to say: "I think the way that the Secret Path is written in the visual, the visuality of the movie or the film allows our [Indigenous] students to learn even more about their own history, but also allows their non-Indigenous peers to learn the true history of Canada."

When Ms. Talaga asked how the students reacted to *Secret Path*, Mr. Baker said: "I think the biggest thing for us in our district is the Secret Path has allowed our Indigenous youth to become more in a leadership role within their classrooms of sharing their story, but also the story of Chanie and how important it is to understand Indian Residential Schools.

"And so, some of our students who were kind of quiet in the classroom and not willing to participate. We've seen success stories where they've become the leaders in various projects within their classroom, to support the [Gord Downie & Chanie Wenjack] Fund, and to support the education."

Ms. Talaga asked how Mr. Baker measured the success of *Secret Path* in the classroom.

"We believe it's working in our district because we measure success by the simple fact of our parents who are continually contacting us in our leadership role saying 'hey, my students are coming home and talking about the Wenjack family, the Gord Downie legacy, or truth and reconciliation, can you support us by giving us resources as adults, to support our children and their learning?'

"That conversation wasn't happening as short as five years ago. So, I believe the fund has helped open the doors for our parent community to learn, also, along with their students, around Indian Residential Schools and truth and reconciliation."

While it is commendable that *Secret Path* has sparked interest in the Indian residential schools, the fact remains that the book provides a false account of 12-year-old Charlie Wenjack's last six days on earth

\* \* \*

Learning Bird is an organization that provides educational resources to 66 schools in seven provinces. An article posted on their website on October 2, 2018, said:

"Since our team took our *Secret Path* boxed set out of its package, we've been big fans. The boxed set includes an album, graphic novel, and animated movie. Gord Downie and Jeff Lemire created a compelling retelling of Chanie Wenjack's story.

"Chanie escaped from residential school and attempted to journey home on a cold winter's night. *Secret Path* has had a tremendous impact on helping Canadians understand the impact of residential schools. It inspired us to create a resource kit, *Storytelling and* Secret Path."

The next section about Charlie Wenjack asks students "to think about what it might feel like to lose language and how powerful it feels to get it back. This handout shows learners what it's like to suddenly lose access to words and how that impacts their communication ability."

It goes on to say: "In Gord Downie's *Secret Path*, Chanie Wenjack repeats this phrase: *'I am a stranger. Do you know what I mean?*. But

Charlie has trouble explaining how he feels, so he just keeps walking. Like thousands of other kids who were sent to live at residential schools across Canada, Chanie's language was taken away from him. These experiences left him without the right words to say what was in his head and heart.

"Language helps us talk about how we feel, tell stories, and connect to each other. This activity will help you and your class see what it might feel like to lose language—and how powerful it feels to get it back."

As we have heard from Marie Loewen, the only time students at Cecilia Jeffrey Indian Residential School were not allowed to use their native language was when they were in the classroom or in the presence of staff.

Further on, the Learning Bird resource kit says: "*Secret Path* is a multi-media project that intends to share the life and experiences of Chanie Wenjack with a wide audience on Turtle Island and around the world."

Learning Bird produced a video analyzing one of Gord Downie's songs from the *Secret Path* album, which it claims "is based on the true story of Chanie Wenjack."

In commenting on *The Stranger* song, Learning Bird asks students to recall that: "Like many children who were taken away from their homes, it makes sense that they felt like strangers, forced to leave behind their language and culture, and assimilate themselves in a new world."

On a November 23, 2016, Learning Bird Radio broadcast, Don Corber, an education specialist at Learning Bird, said *Secret Path* is "all about the true story of a real person named Chanie Wenjack, a 12-year-old Anishinaabe boy who died in 1966 when he tried to run away from the Cecilia Jeffrey Indian Residential School."

Mr. Corber said Cecilia Jeffrey was funded by the federal government "to teach kids like Chanie how to talk, and learn, and live like white Canadians. And how to let go of all the things that their families taught them."

He also said: "We don't know a lot about what happened to Chanie at Cecilia Jeffrey, but we do know that after three years of living in those conditions, Chanie found his chance to escape from the school."

Again, there were no prison-like conditions at the school from which Charlie or any other child would have had reason to "escape."

Mr. Corber claims that Charlie was one of at least 33 Indigenous children who died "while they were running away from their terrible experiences at residential schools.

"But Chanie's story pushed people in the Canadian government and churches to start thinking about the many problems, the injustices, and the dangers of the residential school system."

He said Gord Downie's main goal after being diagnosed with terminal brain cancer was to "share Chanie's story. He wanted to get Canadians listening, learning, and taking action to heal from this history.

"Downie's purpose for the whole project was to honour Chanie's life and the stories of the thousands of kids who went through similar experiences. He wanted to do this for the widest possible audience: all Canadians."

\* \* \*

On January 19, 2019, Deputy Grand Chief Derek Fox of the Nishnawbe Aski Nation, announced that a new curriculum based on *Secret Path* was going to be introduced to schools in Peterborough, Ontario.

"As we launched this curriculum we remember the love and determination of both Chanie Wenjack and Gord Downie, whose individual journeys ended with their legacies intertwined in such a unique and meaningful way to reveal the truth about the Indian Residential School System," Mr. Fox said in a press release.

"We thank the Wenjack and Downie families for supporting the development of this resource that will allow educators and students to understand the tragedy of Residential Schools and the inter-generational effects. We are grateful for their efforts and all those who make worked so hard to make this possible."

Pearl Achneepineskum and Patrick and Mike. Downie were on hand for the launch.

According to a report in the *Peterborough Examiner*, *Secret Path* tells "the story of Chanie Wenjack and his tragic attempt to flee a residential school and find his way home....

"Some Ontario teachers have already incorporated Secret Path in the classroom." The effort was spearheaded in Peterborough by Mitch Champagne, who teaches at Sacred Heart elementary school.

The report referred to the fact that Mr. Champagne had developed a lesson plan in 2017 that incorporated *Secret Path* into the study of residential schools.

"Champagne, who also teaches at Trent, also made the lesson plan available to other teachers across the country," the report said.

\* \* \*

In a column published in newspapers across Canada in March, 2017, WE Charity co-founders Craig and Marc Kielburger said Charlie Wenjack "died **fleeing** [emphasis added] his residential school" and encouraged Canadians to donate money in support of "Legacy Rooms" [now called "Legacy Spaces"] in restaurants, schools, libraries and corporate boardrooms.

"For a $5,000 donation," they wrote, "the Downie-Wenjack Fund will provide an official plaque and signage explaining Chanie's story to set the tone for the Legacy Room. The money raised supports initiatives to teach about residential schools in Canadian classrooms."

Gord Downie gets top billing on the plaques in "Legacy Spaces" sprouting up across Canada. His trademark hat sits atop the words "**The Gord Downie**" in boldface. The line below in smaller, lighter, type says: "& CHANIE WENJACK FUND." There's a photo of Gord Downie performing at one of his concerts on the left side of the plaque and one of a shy, smiling little Chanie on the right.

One might well ask whose "legacy" is being commemorated. Charlie Wenjack's name is completely overshadowed.

The plaque looks like part of a donor-supported promotion for the late Gord Downie's solo albums.

On October 28, 2017, the *Globe and Mail* published an article about a Canada 150 reconciliation journey through the Northwest Passage on the *Polar Prince*.

At one point, Aluki Kotierk, president of Nunavut Tunngavik Inc. broke down in tears during a group discussion on reconciliation in the ship's Legacy Room.

"I just don't know why in this Legacy Room there is no box of Kleenex," she said prompting laughter from her colleagues. "**Or why Gord Downie's name is bigger than Chanie Wenjack's**" on the plaque on the wall.

Good question.

\* \* \*

Mi'kmaq comedienne/broadcaster Candy Palmater provided an Indigenous perspective on Gord Downie being given the Order of Canada in June, 2017, in recognition of his devotion "to promoting dialogue, raising awareness of the history of residential schools and moving the country along the path to reconcilation."

In an article that was published in *Chatelaine* magazine on December 4, 2017, Ms. Palmater said she had been a big fan of Mr. Downie since hearing him and *The Tragically Hip* for the first time on a car radio in 1989.

Ms. Palmater said she had mixed feelings when she first heard that Mr. Downie was releasing an album and graphic novel about Charlie Wenjack's short life and tragic death.

She was glad that he was bringing the issue to the public's attention and thought that it would prove cathartic for the Wenjack family to have Charlie's story "embraced by such a famous Canadian."

However, she then wrote: "But I wasn't sure it was Gord's story to tell. And I predicted, correctly, that Canadians would pay more attention to the story coming from Gord than they did when Indigenous author Lee Maracle wrote about it years earlier."

When Ms. Palmater heard that Mr. Downie was going to receive the Order of Canada, she assumed that it was on account of the significant contribution he and *The Tragically Hip* had made to Canadian music.

And, given that Mr. Downie had been diagnosed with terminal brain cancer, it made sense that the honour be bestowed sooner than later.

"But when I read that he was receiving the Order of Canada not just for music but for his leadership as an Indigenous activist," she wrote. "I was stunned. Surely this was a misprint. After all, I know so many Indigenous people who have given their whole lives to furthering our cause without ever being recognized. Not only that, but so often their lifelong anti-racist work has taken a toll on their health and careers....

"But I was also shocked at the number of articles that referred to him as a leader in Indigenous activism. After Gord died, our Prime Minister said, through tears, that Gord wanted to make Canada better. Well, no disrespect to Gord, but many Indigenous people also want Canada to be better, and have been pushing and working for this ever since [European] contact."

Ms. Palmater said she had been interviewed by CBC TV anchor Peter Mansbridge a few months before her article in *Chatelaine* was published.

"When I mentioned my concern about this [*Secret Path*] subject, Mr. Mansbridge asked: 'You aren't angry at Gord for doing this, are you?' I said: 'No, I'm angry that I live in a country where, still, no one listens until a white man says it'."

Ms. Palmater emphasized in her article that in absolutely no way did she mean to disrespect the late Gord Downie's memory.

"But Canadians need to wake up and realize that collectively feeling bad for little Chanie Wenjack dying on the tracks all those years ago will never change the future for one Indigenous child today.

"Activism is not warm and fuzzy. It is not about embracing a famous person who makes an album about a situation. It is about facing the hard truths that may make you feel uncomfortable. It's about getting out of the way of the Indigenous people who have been demanding change for decades now. It's about realizing you may be part of the problem, and figuring out how to use that knowledge to move toward change....

"I hope, at the very least, that Canadians will re-examine this appetite for white narratives that make them feel comfortable in the 'activism' of pity, while actually remaining removed from the equation. I hope they begin to listen to the Indigenous narratives that make them question all they know and engage in the discomfort of true personal and political activism."

\* \* \*

A headline in the December 10, 2017, issue of *Halifax Today*, said: "Council to look at one-time donation to The Downie Wenjack Legacy Room Project."

The report said Halifax Regional Council would decide at its meeting on December 12, 2017, whether or not to establish a Legacy Room—as the Legacy Spaces were then called—in the main floor boardroom at City Hall and make a one-time $25,000 donation to the Gord Downie & Chanie Wenjack Fund.

The Legacy Room, to include art produced in collaboration with Indigenous artists, would be opened in partnership with the Mi'kmaq community.

"Armbrae Academy, Dalhousie University, Waterfront Development Corporation and Barrington Steakhouse and Oyster Bar have also recently committed to opening similar rooms in Halifax," the report said.

A report in *Halifax Today*, on December 13, 2017, said: "Council voted unanimously Tuesday to install a 'legacy room' at City Hall and make a $25,000 contribution to reconciliation projects under the Gord Downie and Chanie Wenjack Fund."

The report also said: "[Gord] Downie's solo-project 'Secret Path' told the story of Chanie Wenjack, a 12-year-old boy who died of hunger and exposure **trying to escape** [emphasis added] a residential school in Ontario."

"This is an opportunity for us to say that we care about this and we want to learn from it and we want to be part of the solution," Mayor Mike Savage said.

The report said he added that the Legacy Room would also "provide a chance for all residents to learn the story of Wenjack and some of the historic wrongs committed not only in our country, but our own province."

The report also said Councillor David Hendsbee had put forward a motion to defer a decision on the matter "until concerns laid out in an email to council were addressed."

That was in reference to an email I sent to Mayor Savage and all members of Halifax Regional Council on December 11, 2017, drawing their attention to all that was false in *Secret Path*.

The report in *Halifax Today* said: "The details of the concerns weren't laid out publicly but HRM's Indigenous Advisor Wyatt White [who played a key role in getting *Secret Path* into classrooms across Nova Scotia] told council he felt they weren't worth addressing.

"[Councillor] Hendsbee's motion to defer was defeated and Savage's motion carried unanimously."

In an interview with Indigenous Advisor White that was published in *Halifax Today* on December 20, 2017, the interviewer said: "You've been a proponent of the *Secret Path* and last week we saw some pushback during the discussion of a Legacy Room at City Hall to having Gord Downie's name centred. How do you respond to that debate?"

"It was never intended to be a source document," Mr. White replied. "It's an artistic representation between two artists—two white artists—based on a third representation, the *Macleans* article.

"People shouldn't be looking to the Secret Path as anything more than the inspiration for reconciliation. Because it's one of the few really big examples of reconciliation, people automatically attribute more to it than is required.

"If we had lots and lots of resources in the school system telling what would be the thousands and thousands of other stories of kids who didn't make it, we wouldn't be having the conversation about why does it take the guy of European descent who's famous to tell somebody else's story?"

# Chapter 18

**On October 30, 2019**, CBC news reported that a book by Canadian author Tanya Talaga which included a chapter on Charlie Wenjack was going to be mandatory reading for Grade 11 students in Windsor, Ontario, and Essex County.

The report said the school board had made a decision in 2016 to develop an Indigenous protocol in response to the recommendations of the $60 million Truth and Reconciliation Commission of Canada.

Eight of the 15 high schools in the Windsor area had replaced Grade 11 English course materials with books by Indigenous authors, including Ms. Talaga's *Seven Fallen Feathers*.

According to the CBC report, the new course was called Understanding Contemporary First Nations, Métis and Inuit Voices.

The report said: "English teachers who are affected by the course changes spend a year learning the new novels before teaching them to their students."

On January 17, 2020, a report in the *Ottawa Citizen* said that students at the Ottawa Catholic School Board "are ditching Shakespeare and Margaret Attwood in favour of studying literature by Indigenous authors like Richard Wagamese and Tanya Talaga...The board has approved a change from the traditional course to an offering called 'English: Understanding Contemporary First Nations, Métis, and Inuit Voices'," the report said.

Five secondary schools were already offering the course and all of the Ottawa Catholic School Board's schools would have it within two years.

"A similar change has been adopted or is underway at several other boards across the province as they try to increase the diversity of literature being studied and implement recommendations of Canada's Truth and Reconciliation Commission," the report said.

A report from board staff that had been accepted by the trustees that week said the switch to Indigenous authors "allows students to see our history through an Indigenous lens" and offers students a "different story—one that is pertinent to the history of our country."

Let's take a look at how Ms. Talaga's *Seven Fallen Feathers* portrays Charlie's tragic death and what life was like at Ceciia Jeffrey Indian Residential School.

Ms. Talaga mistakenly claims that the school was operated by the United Church of Canada and that there was "a revolving door to the principal's position—mostly all United Church ministers."

In fact, the original school at Shoal Lake, about 70 kilometres west of Kenora, was opened in 1902 by the Presbyterian Church in Canada—23 years before the United Church was established.

The United Church of Canada was founded in 1925 in a merger involving the Methodist Church of Canada, the Congregational Union of Ontario and Quebec, the Association of Local Union Churches and two-thirds of the Presbyterian Church in Canada.

The new United Church of Canada took control of nine of the 11 Indian residential schools the Presbyterian Church had been operating.

However, the Presbyterian Church retained control of Cecilia Jeffrey Indian Residential School and the school in Birtle, Manitoba.

Ms. Talaga says: "By 1924, the United Church and the Department of Indian Affairs were actively discussing building another school closer to Kenora."

In fact, the United Church of Canada did not exist in 1924. The discussions that resulted in the move to Kenora in 1929 were between the Presbyterian Church and Indian Affairs.

When I raised this issue with former senior staffers Abe Loewen and George MacMillan, they told me the United Church had absolutely nothing to do with Cecilia Jeffrey Indian Residential School.

All employees were hired and paid by the Presbyterian Church in Canada. All correspondence and reports were addressed to officials of the Presbyterian Church.

Ms. Talaga says she was shown a collection of pictures of students at Cecilia Jeffrey by someone who had a mobile office on the old school site. "Nobody looks happy," she wrote. "The boys look miserable cold and uncomfortable." She went on to say: "looking at these pictures makes me feel as though I am disturbing a gravesite."

As you might recall from what I wrote earlier, Cecilia Jeffrey was described in a very positive manner in more than 300 letters students and parents wrote between 1958 and 1966. I have seen many unposed pictures of happy, smiling children at the school where many said they felt loved and cared for.

Commenting on photos taken at Christmas time, Ms. Talaga writes: "The images of Indigenous children sitting around artificial Christmas trees, full of plastic lights and red and green plastic ornaments, **are among the most disturbing** [emphasis added]. Some of them are passing around gifts. They would have likely been taught about Christmas, but for many of the kids this was the white man's tradition, not theirs."

Ms. Talaga's claim that Christmas was a foreign experience for the children would come as a surprise to the many parents who wrote "God bless you" at the end of their letters.

As you will recall from having read the letters, parents said they prayed for the staff and their children and asked Principal Robinson to remember them in his prayers.

"May God bless you. A happy merry Christmas to you. Happy new year," one parent wrote. "We always pray for you," wrote another.

And then there's the parent who wrote: "I hope that they pray on Christmas. I guess I will want them to come home in summer because it's too far from here to send them home for Christmas."

Most of the parents—including Charlie Wenjack's father who was an Elder at the local Anglican church—were practising Christians. In fact, as far back as 1921, Statistics Canada reported that 90% of the residents at Charlie's home reserve were Anglican or Roman Catholic.

Ms. Talaga seems unaware of the fact that thousands of Indigenous people had converted to Christianity decades before those "disturbing" photos were taken of children celebrating Christmas at Cecilia Jeffrey.

It is totally inappropriate for her to claim that students celebrating Christmas at Cecilia Jeffrey Indian Residential School in the 1960's were participating in "the white man's tradition, not theirs."

Ms. Talaga claims that, at the time Charlie was at the school, the senior girls spent half the day "doing housework and crafts, some worked under the nurses in the dispensary. The boys in grades four to eight also attended classes, then worked the other half of the day doing general farm work, interior and exterior decorating and painting, as well as scrubbing, sweeping and dusting. There were also small cleaning duties and farm work for both boys and girls before and after school."

In fact, as we learned earlier, most of the students spent the day at public schools in Kenora. None of them did any farm work. The barn burned down in 1954, nine years before Charlie arrived at the school, and was not replaced.

Ms. Talaga says: "A high, barbed-wire fence snaked around the perimeter of Cecilia Jeffrey. At the back of the school there was an opening in the fence, a path to the outside world."

There was no high barbed-wire fence surrounding the Cecilia Jeffrey property. And, as we have already seen, there was no fence or outside gate to prevent the children from wandering away whenever they felt like it. The school was not a prison.

"When groups of students ran away," Ms. Talaga wrote, "it was because of the abuse they were facing at the school." The children who called the principal and his wife "Mom" and "Dad", signed their letters to them "Love" and thanked them for being such good parents to them, would most likely have taken issue with that unsubstantiated claim.

"The abuse suffered at the hands of the adult supervisors took its toll on the students," Ms. Talaga wrote. "They became further disengaged from the classroom, angry, and in need of someone to take their rage out on. For some of these kids, the younger children were easy victims. This is the life Chanie ran from."

There is no evidence to support this claim.

Ms. Talaga goes on to say: "It was on a Sunday, October 16, 1966, that Chanie decided enough was enough. He discussed the idea of running away with his buddies Ralph and Jackie MacDonald."

There is no evidence, anywhere, of Charlie being the one to initiate the decision to leave the school that sunny afternoon. Ralph McDonald was clearly the dominant male in the group. And, as the inquest jury was told, it was Ralph who initiated the decision to leave. Charlie simply tagged along.

Ms. Talaga says something must have been going on that Sunday afternoon because "nine students tried to escape. Maybe they knew the weather would soon turn and if they were going to make a break for it, it would be now or never."

Later in the book, she says: "A critical mass of kids all running, could not have been a coincidence. They must have been running from something."

However, as the letters clearly show, neither the students nor their parents considered Cecilia Jeffrey to be a prison from which any student would have found it necessary to "escape".

In an article published in the *Toronto Star* on September 11, 2016, Ms. Talaga wrote that "[Charlie] Wenjack could not take one more second at the Presbyterian-run residential school."

There is no evidence to support that claim.

After writing about Charlie's body being found, Ms. Talaga wrote: "But no one thought to call Wenjack's parents. They were not notified when he ran away or immediately told when he died."

As you might recall, five of Charlie's sisters and his mother were informed of his death within twenty-four hours of his body being identified. Meanwhile, police were trying to contact his father, who was out on his trapline, by radio phone.

In *Seven Fallen Feathers,* Ms. Talaga writes that Charlie's eldest sister, Daisy Munroe, remembers that Charlie's father refused to eat or talk "for days." When he did leave the house, she wrote, "it was because he had something to do. He needed to dig his son's grave.

"When he was finished, he officiated the funeral and gave the service."

This account is completely at odds with what Principal Colin Wasacase wrote at the time in his letter to the Women's Missionary Society. The burial took place on the same day that the coffin arrived—not after Charlie's father refused to eat or talk "for days." The funeral service was conducted by the Anglican minister who had joined them at Nakina.

Most of what Ms. Talaga writes about Charlie and his sisters in the book that is required reading for thousands of Canadian children cannot be substantiated.

However, neither the children nor their parents have any way of knowing that.

# Chapter 19

**AUTHOR JOSEPH BOYDEN** claims that Charlie Wenjack told him what to write in his 102-page pocketbook *Wenjack*, which is also being used in the classrooms.

In an interview on TVO's *The Agenda* that aired on November 1, 2016, he said: "I don't know if it's so much I decided to tell his story or that he decided for me to tell it. He so strongly spoke to me and he spoke to Gord [Downie] obviously and a number of other people. He just wouldn't let me go.

"When it came time to write something his voice started speaking to me. His voice came through so strong it was as if he was saying 'I don't want to be gone yet. Don't forget me.' He's telling me what to say.

"To capture his voice was one of those rare moments for a writer where it just floats me and so I just listened. I listened carefully. He's telling me what he needed to say."

In an interview with *Globe and Mail* columnist Denise Balkissoon published on October 18, 2016, Mr. Boyden said: "This kid Charlie, whose real name was Chanie, his teachers couldn't pronounce his name or they didn't care to, he's such a symbol. This beautiful little 12-year-old, shy boy, he ran away from school, his family tells me, because he was being sexually abused. It's disgusting."

Mr. Boyden, who said he had read Ian Adams' 1967 article about Charlie in *Maclean's*, said: "He couldn't take it anymore so he ran. Four days later he was found dead on the tracks." As you might recall, Charlie did not run away and it was actually seven days.

*Wenjack* was the strongest writing he'd ever done, Mr. Boyden said. "It was as if I was being channelled when I wrote that book. Chanie's voice came to me very quickly."

He said he incorporated spirits of the forest who took the forms of animals in the book to describe things Charlie couldn't tell him about. "These different voices of the different spirits following him and watching him on his journey allowed me as the writer to explain the bigger picture going on."

When he got close to completing the book, Mr. Boyden said to himself "this is a story that I want people to read in high school and in college. I want parents to sit down with their children at the proper age and be able to read it."

A publisher's note from Simon & Schuster Canada said Charlie "realizes too late" just how far away his home is. Spirits of the forest offer him comfort "on his difficult journey back to the place he was so brutally removed from."

The back cover of the book is illustrated with the skull of a mouse, captioned: "One day I will run. One day they won't hurt me anymore."

In the author's note, Mr. Boyden said Charlie was "forcibly" taken from his home when he was nine. "None of them knew how long he'd be gone. Chanie came home two years later in a casket."

At the risk of appearing to nitpick, it was actually **three** years. Accuracy is important in a book that is being presented to school children as a true story. Let's take a closer look at Joseph Boyden's *Wenjack*.

On the first page of the book, he has Charlie saying: "My friends, the two [McDonald] brothers, call the pale teacher Fish Belly or sometimes Sucker Belly. They don't say it to his face because he's strong and he smells like what the colour yellow or maybe brown smells like, and he has a room in the basement that scares the life from us."

On the next page, Mr. Boyden writes: "If the Fish Bellies [teachers] hear me speak my [Ojibway] words they beat me with a stick and make me eat soap."

As you will recall, Marie Loewen said the children were free to speak Ojibway or Oji-Cree in the dormitories and out on the playground. The only time they had to speak English was when they were in the classroom or in the presence of a teacher or member of the staff.

Mr. Boyden writes about Charlie knowing when kids had run away and been caught because of the "long red marks" on their backs. Former staff are firm in saying that absolutely did **not** happen. "One day I will run," Charlie says. "One day they won't hurt me anymore."

On Page 5, Mr. Boyden says Charlie and the McDonald brothers didn't plan to run away that day. "It was the older of the two brothers who said to his younger sibling and Charlie that they should go visit an uncle who would take them out on the traplines so that the school people they called Fish Bellies would never find them again.

"A dozen children had run away from the school that week but all had been captured and returned and beaten."

Mr. Boyden is correct in saying it was Ralph McDonald who initiated the decision to run, or walk, away. However, there is no evidence to support his claim that 12 children were captured and beaten that week.

Like Gord Downie, Jeff Lemire and Tanya Talaga, Mr. Boyden appears to feel it's okay to make things up as he goes along.

He says the three boys "climbed the fence" when they knew no member of the school staff was looking. As you might recall from my examination of the photos, there was no fence there. And, as Ian Adams wrote in *Maclean's*, "slipping away was simple".

Instead of having the three boys spend the first night at "Mr. Benson's" cabin, as the *Maclean's* article which he claims to have read says, Mr. Boyden has them shivering in the cold out in the bush.

"The three **brown** [emphasis added] children buffet along the swollen rivers of sleep," he wrote. "Their bodies clutching each other for warmth. They shake in half sleep despite holding on to a friend or a brother.

"When they awake, though, they will feel the shame of having touched one another, if even just for warmth. This lesson not taught by their own but by others will by morning dissipate with the early frost."

He then has Charlie say: "The brothers don't look at me as they rise to run, and I don't feel bad. I can feel they are no longer mad at me for what I don't know I did. I think they don't know, too."

Nothing that was written at the time, or since, supports Mr. Boyden's account of the boys waking up feeling "the shame of having touched one another".

In describing a journey to the uncle's cabin through dense forest—in fact, they followed Highway 658—Mr. Boyden has them squatting on their haunches and chewing thin red willow shoots whenever they stop for a rest.

"Every time I catch up," Charlie says, "they stand from squatting and spit the twigs from their mouths and disappear again." At one point on the way to the cabin, Charlie says: "The younger one has joined the older and both squat and chew on sticks and stare down the path they will take."

*Why in the world would Mr. Boyden have Ojibway boys in 1966 squatting on their haunches chewing twigs? What are children reading* Wenjack *in 2023 to make of it?*

As the boys get close to a river, Charlie says: "The Fish Belly who teaches us doesn't let us drink any water when we answer words wrong. He doesn't let us eat either. I'm used to hungry me. But I can't get used to no water."

The forest spirit animals Mr. Boyden used to tell his distorted version of Charlie's story included a sucker fish, a crow, a hummingbird, owl, pike, spider, wood tick, beaver, snow goose, rabbit, and a lynx

At one point, the wood tick and some others watch as Charlie wakes up in Charles Kelly's cabin wanting to be helpful but not knowing what to do.

"The only thing the school he's run from has taught him." Mr. Boyden wrote, "is how to be fearful of adults." That certainly conflicts with the way the school was described in the more than 300 positive letters written by students and parents.

When Clara Kelly wakes up, Mr. Boyden wrote, her husband told her he was going to take the nephews to the trapline to see if they could get some food to put on their bare table and would be gone for a week. In fact. they returned home the next morning. Mr. Kelly only went to Mud Lake to check on his trapline.

"Your job," Mr. Boyden quotes him saying as he points to Charlie, "is to send the stranger away. Someone broke something in him. We don't have the tools to fix it. Send him back to the school. Or find out where he lives and send him there. Give him a little food for the journey."

Given that there is nothing in the *Maclean's* article Mr. Boyden says he read and that he didn't start writing *Wenjack* until 48 years after the event, it's clear that he made up the words he put in Mr. Kelly's mouth.

It's worth noting that there's no mention of best friend Eddie Cameron in Mr. Boyden's account. He says only the two McDonald brothers were with Charlie at the Kellys' main cabin. In fact, Eddie Cameron was there also. That's in the *Maclean's* article.

And then, after Mr. Kelly and his nephews leave for the trapline, Mr. Boyden invents a scene between one of the Kellys' daughters and Charlie.

"The girl lies in her bed and stares at this strange boy," he wrote. "She can see something in him she thinks. Someone hurt him bad. So bad that it is stuck inside him and he's so scared of it but more scared to let it out…He sees she stares at him but she won't move her eyes. She dares him with her dark eyes to tell her why he hurts."

Again, this is a figment of Mr. Boyden's vivid imagination.

Contrary to the article in *Maclean's,* Mr. Boyden has Charles Kelly telling Charlie he must leave immediately after Mr. Kelly and his nephews arrived at the trapline by canoe. "You can't stay here," the uncle says. "You must return to the school."

As Charlie walks along the railway tracks, Mr. Boyden writes, he hears the sound of a beaver's tail hitting the water. It reminds him of "the slap of the teacher across my face. The other children stare at me. I spoke out loud in the class in my tongue because I forgot what Nindede [his father] warned me."

He recalls having intended to speak English, but spoke in Ojibway out of habit. "I am sorry I say, and he slaps me again so I fall out of my chair. I mean't [sic] to say it in English, I try to tell him, but my tongue came out instead. I'm sorry I say from the floor. He thinks I make fun and he grips my hair in his fist and drags me out the room and down some stairs and to the dark basement that scares us all to dying."

It goes without saying that this simply just did **not** happen. There is no mention of anything like it in the 1967 article in *Maclean's* or in the local newspaper's report on the inquest.

Mr. Boyden says the teacher took a key from a metal ring on his waist, unlocked the door and shoved Charlie into the room. There's a skinny mattress on the floor covered in yellow stains. The teacher tells Charlie to take his clothes off. When Charlie is naked, the teacher picks up the clothes, leaves the room and locks the door.

Charlie shivers in the dark, trying not to cry. The door opens and he sees the tall shadow staring down at him. "He lies down beside me on the skinny mattress that smells of old pee and he takes me in his arms and holds me. His skin is gizhaate. Hot. His skin glows like a fish belly in the dark. Ozhaawaa.

"He pushes himself against me. He smells like the colour called brown. He pushes me on my stomach. His mouth. Nindoon. On my back. Nipikwan. Hurt. He hurts. Don't hurt me. Please don't hurt."

In reading this sordid account, it's worth remembering Mr. Boyden saying that Charlie told him what to write in the book, that he "channelled" him.

As with the pedophile priest in *Secret Path*, there is no credible evidence to support Mr. Boyden's graphic description of Charlie being sodomized by a teacher. Like much of what he wrote in *Wenjack*, he just made it up.

*Why couldn't he simply tell Charlie's story as we know it from the accounts that were written at the time? Where's the benefit to the school children who are reading this stuff?*

As Charlie stumbles along the C.N.R. tracks, Mr. Boyden writes that he "is right in remembering his family lives near the railroad tracks by big shining water but what he does not fully understand is that home is hundreds of miles away."

In fact, Charlie's home at the remote fly-in community of Ogoki Post is nowhere near the railway tracks. It's about an hour's flight northeast of the train station at Nakina.

Mr. Boyden writes about a forest spirit in the form of a lynx coming across Charlie's lifeless body lying beside the tracks.

"As the snow falls thicker, she wraps him more tightly to her so that he may feel again, and with the first true snow of the season falling now, whipped by the wind through the canyon cut out of rock, the mother lynx waltzes Chanie warm in her fur-clad arms and into the forest away from the tracks."

Mr. Boyden writes about the engineer on the westbound freight spotting Charlie's body beside the tracks just before noon Sunday and notifying the authorities. He notes that officials came to retrieve his body.

"And when it's convenient," he writes, "which turns out to be weeks later, their notification to the deceased's family will be the return of said deceased in a thin casket, remains enclosed, back to his people and to his home."

Charlie's mother was notified of his death less than 24 hours after Principal Colin Wasacase identified his body. His coffin, accompanied by his mother and sisters, Colin Wasacase and the Anglican minister from Nakina, arrived at Ogoki Post two days later.

Mr. Boyden's claim that the family wasn't notified until "weeks later" is totally bogus.

The last paragraph of Mr. Boyden's book has Charlie dancing in the forest with the spirits in animal form who have followed his fateful journey along the railway tracks. "We watch the boy warm in our presence, watch him dance and eat and share his shy smile, his dark eyes turned darker and sparkling."

Joseph Boyden is a very talented writer. He could have written a worthwhile book of fiction based on Charlie Wenjack's tragic story. But that's not the way he described his book. He said he set out to recount Charlie's last journey. "He's telling me what to say," he claimed. He uses Charlie's name throughout the book and, to a large extent, he follows the sequence of events pretty much in the way they were described at the time.

However, as with Lee Maracle's *Sojourner's Truth and Other Stories,* Gord Downie's *Secret Path* and Tanya Talaga's *Seven Fallen Feathers,* Joseph Boyden's *Wenjack,* turns out to be yet another fabricated account claiming to be a true story.

Our children deserve better. Much better.

And parents have a right, and responsibility, to know the extent to which their children are being misinformed in our schools.

# Chapter 20

**IN CLOSING THIS** book let me share with you what three Ojibways from northwestern Ontario told me about the horrors they experienced at Indian residential schools when I interviewed them in 1996 and 1997.

On finishing Grade 8 at St. Mary's Indian Residential School in Kenora, Fred Kelly—Yes, the same Fred Kelly who organized the protest march in Kenora in November, 1965—was shipped several hundred kilometres away from home to the St. Paul's High School at Lebret, Saskatchewan, which was operated by the Oblate Fathers. Lebret is a tiny community at the eastern end of Mission Lake, about 70 kilometres northeast of Regina.

Why go several hundred kilometres west to Saskatchewan in order to get your high school education?

"Apparently, it was just simply unthinkable for us to go to a public school and the rationale being, as far as the churches were concerned, they wanted to see our [Catholic] religion intact and to keep me from falling prey to the evils of society, whatever the hell that was," Mr. Kelly replied.

"My continuous rebellion [to the officials at Indian Affairs] was, 'explain to me why I cannot go to any of these high schools in town [Kenora]?' It was never discussed. It was just because you cannot. Simply the answer was because you cannot go and we're going to send you where we think is best for you. So I went to Lebret."

All of the letters Mr. Kelly sent to his family at his home reserve of Sabaskong, about 150 kilometres southeast of Kenora, were censored by the school authorities. So were any letters sent to him by his mother or other family members.

In its 1889 *Rules and Regulations for Industrial Schools*, the Department of Indian Affairs directed that, while Indigenous children were to be allowed to write to their parents **twice a year**, their letters as well as all incoming mail "must be scrutinized by the Principal before transmission or delivery."

"I would imagine it was to keep out outside influences," Mr. Kelly suggested. "Don't forget that when residential schools were set up, and I didn't know about this until later on when I found out some of the policies, the residential schools were based on total assimilation.

"Duncan Campbell Scott, [the Deputy Superintendent General of Indian Affairs from 1913 to 1932] said in the House of Commons when he announced the residential school system something to the effect of this is the best system that's going to be there and it is going to be implemented until not one body, until not one Indian, remains that has not been absorbed into the Canadian polity. So it was based on assimilation, obviously.

"And that's putting it kindly. I'm talking about cultural genocide here because you were talking about a system of the *Indian Act* that was so oppressive that forced the kids to be taken into school.

"The [white] Indian agent was the person who was in charge of enforcing the *Indian Act*. You needed permission to leave the reservation and he could enforce the law in that way, so he was also judge and jury and also the enforcer. Check these out in the *Indian Act* and it's quite clear the powers that he had and that was the judicial system on reserve, remnants of which we still see and so to that extent, by going at the parents, if you were not in school, they could go after the parents and literally force them by law.

"When the family allowances [a monthly payment to Canadian families with children regardless of income] were later to be instituted [in 1945] and being applicable as universal, then the *Indian Act* was also amended so that people could not receive family allowances if their kids were not in school. So they used that *Indian Act* and coercion among the parents to force their kids into school. Those that defied that were, in fact, jailed or charged.

"Such was the power of the Indian agent, such was the power of the Department of Indian Affairs who then worked in co-operation with the churches to carry out this policy and thus the residential school system. Most of them were established somewhere around the turn of the century and I believe St. Mary's [in Kenora] was established in 1902, 1903, somewhere in there."

Fred Kelly believed that the British Government had a "detribalization policy" in Canada and in Africa and that the purpose of that policy was to wipe out the tribal system. Stop it dead in its tracks.

"When we say it kindly, we say assimilation. But the downright policy was extermination which is cultural genocide, by extermination. Let me give you an example. One of the Indian agents at the time, Duncan Campbell Scott, speaking in support of this residential school policy said, 'the best thing that we can do for these Indian people is to educate the savagery out of them, therefore, we must take them away from their parents, isolate them.'"

Mr. Kelly quoted Mr. Scott saying. "Secondly, they must not speak their language. If we wish to remove them from their culture, we must remove them from their language."

That's why he couldn't speak Ojibway in the school system, Mr. Kelly said. "Remove them from their culture, remove them from our customs and our traditions and our own sacred beliefs."

Despite the unrelenting efforts of the Sisters and Fathers to drum it out of him, Fred Kelly held on to his own language during the unhappy days he spent in the Indian residential school system.

"I've never lost my language and that was a struggle," he said rather proudly.

Nevertheless, he did suffer the emotional and physical abuse that was so often an inescapable part of attending many of the Indian residential schools the Canadian government had established.

"The indoctrination of the residential school system did not suit me well, did not suit me. I didn't like the indoctrination, the regimentation, the brainwashing. I got beaten up, my head bashed, kicked, beaten up time and again, physically, emotionally and all the time I felt that, and the outcome was, I was stuttering at the time and I didn't know why and I didn't even know what it was called.

"The emotional turmoil of being in a residential school had to come out in some way or another in what is, might be known as, aberrations of behaviour. Some would wet the bed, some would be reticent, some would just withdraw. I would stutter. Other people would just outright be defiant and cause greater abuse to themselves. It's an emotional release and, in my case it was an emotional result, because I obviously don't stutter now and shortly after I left, I didn't stutter anymore."

Two years after arriving at Lebret, Saskatchewan, Fred Kelly was kicked out of the Indian residential school.

"When I went back for my grade 11, they told me 'no, you're not going back. Words were left over here that you and two other people that you hang around with will not be readmitted.'

"Already I was known as a renegade, a ringleader and the words that kept echoing through my mind all through these years was, 'You're very bright. If only we could challenge you', time and again. It's what I went through all the time."

As the train chugged east through the wheat fields of Saskatchewan and Manitoba, Mr. Kelly thought at first that he might as well quit school and head back to his home reserve of Sabaskong.

"But I said, 'no. I'm going to do something with myself.'"

When he got off the train in Kenora at 11:30 at night, the boys' supervisor from St. Mary's Indian Residential School was there to meet him.

"I should say, he and I did not get along well even before. We just did not get along. I didn't want to be near him. He probably didn't want to be near me either, but I guess he had the ulterior motive. He was trying to maintain his hockey team at St. Mary's and I was a goaltender."

The boys' supervisor invited him to stay at the school that night and take a bus to Sabaskong in the morning. He'd have a place to sleep and something to eat.

"On the way there, he told me a few things that really intrigued me. We weren't allowed to have girlfriends, but he mentioned to me this [Mohawk] girl from Maniwaki [about 135 kilometres north of

Ottawa]. She was back. Enticement! And, he said, 'this year we're going to repeat the Chapple Cup Championship and we'd like to have you on the team.'"

Fred Kelly spent the night at St. Mary's and, sure enough, the girlfriend *was* there along with some of the friends he used to hang out with. He decided that he might just as well stay at St. Mary's.

"Could be fun. I don't know. I don't know, but now it was getting kind of late in the year. It's already the middle of September. I said, well, what the hell if I don't like it I can leave at any time. Anyway, I stayed."

He found it a bit odd that, having been kicked out of Lebret because of the indoctrination, the regimentation, the brainwashing, here he was coming back to a residential school. "That's the irony of it."

As was the case at Lebret, all correspondence between the students at St. Mary's and the outside world was censored by the officials in charge of the schools.

"I couldn't even write to my mother without it being censored, so, there was a way around that. I started writing letters to the Department of Indian Affairs and their regional office was in North Bay and I complained about the curriculum [at St. Mary's] in comparison even to Lebret. My idea was why don't we open up our students so they can go to the school of their choice just like everybody else?

"All through this year I wrote about four or five letters and complained about the curriculum, the teaching methodology and here's a case in point. In Lebret, we took French about three times a week. We had a better chance of learning it and it was conversational French.

"In St. Mary's, now I'm in grade 11, doing grade 11 in St. Mary's, we take French half an hour before recess. Then you have recess then afterwards you come and spend the rest of the Friday afternoon doing art, free drawing. So I complained about those kinds of things.

"My average at the end of Grade 11 was astounding. High 90s, 98 something like that and everybody thought I was a genius and without even studying. I knew otherwise. Why? Because of the stuff I had learnt in Lebret, which only goes up to grade 12.

"So you come to grade 11 [at St. Mary's] and it's almost like a repetition. Very, very, little studying and I rack up this mark and I come first without any people even seeing me study. 'This guy's a genius.' No. He's not a genius. It was just the background and what they're teaching you. Because the emphasis here [at St. Mary's] was hockey and church in varying orders, but not education."

Eventually, a guidance counsellor from the Ontario office of Indian Affairs in Toronto came to St. Mary's to interview Mr. Kelly. He said that he wanted to find out what the students wanted to do with their lives and how the school could help them.

"He came to me and came to this part and he said, 'so what should we talk about? Well, why don't we find out first of all what you would like to do and learn, as a profession, as a career'. I said 'well, I'm bored. I don't know.'"

And then the counsellor cut to the chase and got down to the real reason he was there—to follow up on the complaints Mr. Kelly had made about the low standard of education at St. Mary's.

"That's when I said. 'Am I in trouble?' 'No, but somebody is. Is there truth to this?'"

Mr. Kelly made some suggestions about matters worthy of further investigation and left it at that. When he went home to Sabaskong that summer, he expected that he'd be going back to do grade 12.

"The week before school started in September, a priest came to me and said 'I want you to serve my mass.' I definitely had to serve the mass and the only reason I had to serve mass for a year is because St. Mary's was no longer offering Grade 12 and it was my fault.

"I went back to the school and he met with us. The hockey team had won the championship for the second year in a row [with Mr. Kelly as the goalie]. And the principal came and he said, 'we have a decision for you [Indigenous students] to make. St. Mary's will not be offering grade 12 thanks to somebody amongst us who will remain nameless.' Of course, we all knew, the kids knew.

"'And we've made some alternate arrangements. You will be going to school in St. Charles' College in Sudbury.' Sudbury? [about 1,500 kilometres east of Kenora] 'And the train leaves tomorrow at seven o'clock. So I'll let you guys talk about that and then I'll come back.'"

The principal left them for about half an hour and then he came back and asked 'any questions?' "Of course you would have questions. I said 'Why Sudbury? Why not Kenora High School? Why not Fort Frances High School? Nine of these guys come from Fort Frances [about 215 kilometres southeast of Kenora], why can't they go to Fort Frances high school? Why can't I go to Kenora High School?'

"He made it clear it was St. Charles College in Sudbury or back on the reserve. So I told the guys 'well, I guess the die is cast' and away we go to Sudbury, just to hang together. We were there for a month and the principal called us and we had made the football team and getting ready for football, or hockey and the principal called us in and he says, 'I'm calling you guys in together because you came in together and you do seem to do things together. You play football together again and you're making a very fine contribution here, but here's the news.

"'We received a transcript of your marks and we received the background of your education and the sad news is you're going to have to do Grade 12 in two years or take it in one year and pray like mad that you can pass it. Reasonably do it in two years but that means no sports.'"

Mr. Kelly's mother didn't even know he was in Sudbury. His brother John was attending teachers' college in North Bay and he didn't know either.

"The guys looked at me and said, 'what do we do?' I said, 'what do you guys want to do?' I said, for me I gotta go talk to my brother in North Bay. 'What are you going to do?' Two people stayed and did their grade 12 in two years. The rest dropped out, went to work for the steel mill. One guy tried out for the Sudbury Wolves Juniors and he made it. Two went to Dorset and the Ranger School [at the 660,830 square kilometre wilderness area of Algonquin Provincial Park] and I went to North Bay and for the first time I thought here was freedom looking at me. I talked to my brother and I said, 'here are the choices. What do you think I should do?'

"He was going to Teachers' College. And he said, 'well, I'm here, I didn't even know you were anywhere near here. I was a thousand miles away from you guys.' I said, 'Mom doesn't even know I'm here.' Anyway, he said, 'now that you're here, why not go to school here, live with me?' Hey, tremendous idea. So I stayed."

\* \* \*

Annie Wilson was forbidden to speak Ojibway during the five painful years she spent at St. Margaret's Indian Residential School at the Couchiching reserve on the outskirts of Fort Frances, Ontario.

Like many of Canada's residential schools, St. Margaret's was an imposing, four-storey, building. It was built on the Canadian side of the Rainy River, across from International Falls, Minnesota. Our Lady of Lourdes Roman Catholic Church was immediately adjacent to the school.

Ms. Wilson, who was seventy-one when I interviewed her in 1997 at her home at Rainy River First Nations, held on to her language despite the efforts of the white nuns to erase it from her memory.

"The nun would make me stand up and say 'I'll not speak my language again' if I got caught speaking my language," she told me. "That's what she would make me do. 'I'll not speak my language', from nine o'clock till midnight at night I had to repeat that. From nine in the evening till midnight, I had to repeat that for a whole month. That was my punishment for speaking my language. And, at the back of my mind, I said 'No. It's going to stay there.'

"So I got out of the boarding school just in time. I was only there for about five years. It didn't take anything away from me, but I knew I would've lost my language if I would've stayed a little longer. I got out just to keep my language at that time. I almost was forgetting the things that I was taught, the things that I was told by my grandparents. Yeah, they taught me a lot, a lot of things because they took me all over. They took me to all those rituals. I understood everything.

"Everywhere you went, there was a sweat lodge because the sweat lodge was your teacher of all the environment, the nature, and you learnt a lot of this and because you were cleaning yourself as you were learning from the sweat.

"Your sweat helped you remember things, remember everything, how it feels to go through a learning, like sort of like wisdom. You have to say a few things when you were in there. People had to hear you talk about your spirituality or whatever, whatever you were comfortable with you had to talk about. You didn't go in there just because you were to get clean or whatever. You had to go in there and say something."

Ms. Wilson wished that the young people of 1967 could have had a taste of the good life that was lost.

"My grandparents made their own butter as I remember doing this with cream and stuff like that and us kids used to do that and then we'd weed the gardens in the summer time as kids. Kids were told to do things at that time. I don't know today, it's so hard for a child to do anything for nothing. It's not like a long time ago. To me, a long time ago, when you were being taught, you felt that you were being loved.

"Today it's not like that. The loving is misunderstood I think. That's the way I feel sometimes is a misunderstanding. How do you love what's conditional?

"When I was growing up as a child, when I seen people working at home, like my grandfather, my grandmother working together, I thought well this felt like I was loved because I was being taught something that I was going to be able to do something with. The way I used to hear it when I was younger, it was a beautiful life before they were disturbed by any people, like the white people."

While she believed that it was important to get back to the old ways, the traditional ways of the Ojibway, she said that couldn't be done if people couldn't speak the language.

"I think if we get back on our own it will be a better way, but the language has to come in also. The language has to be understood by the younger people so they'll all carry on the traditions of how life was supposed to be."

Ms. Wilson was emphatic about the benefits she enjoyed as a result of being able to speak Ojibway, as a child and as an adult.

"The way I felt when I was a child there was a lot of sharing. Today there's no sharing. The kids don't understand what you're saying because we have to speak in English. They don't know the language. If they knew that language, honest to God, those people would be very smart. They don't know what they're missing. I really feel sorry for them. That's what I tell them in schools when I talk to kids. You missed what I went through when I was a child. I seen love, I seen caring, I seen how things grow.

"You will never see that. You will never be taught the things that I was taught. That will never be in the school neither. But what I went through, when I come out of that boarding school, I was taught to have a garden, taught to go trapping, understand the animals, oodles of stuff. That's when my education started—when I came back out of the crazy school."

Ms. Wilson told me about the times in the early 1990s when she would travel long distances to counsel suicidal young Ojibways, one of whom had made three attempts at taking his own life.

"It's not tradition to kill anybody or commit suicide," she said. "You never reach your grandmother when you commit suicide. No. Because it's not a natural death. A natural death is better than taking your own life. You're disobeying the Creator so you don't get there.

"That's how I teach the kids when they're suicidal. That you're not going to see your mother. Your mother died a year ago and you want to commit suicide because you don't have a mother. 'Why die,' I said, 'why kill yourself when you're not going to see her anyway?'

"The Creator didn't say to take your life. Keep it to help somebody and then go when you're finished. That's what the teachings are. You don't take your own life, I say, and think that you're going to go to a good place. You'll never get there. You'll just go. You're just out of this world, but your spirit doesn't have a home. You suffer."

Ms. Wilson told the young people that everyone has to suffer a bit in life. "That's why the Creator gives us those trials, to see how strong we are. And we can get stronger because of death, because of grief and the grief is not supposed to last a year. It's only supposed to last a few days, till the body goes in the ground and is covered."

In a traditional Ojibway burial, a hole is drilled in the lid of the coffin just by the head so that, after four days, the spirit can leave the body.

"You live and you never forget that, but still you live. You have to live a different life. You got to take what is good. You don't take the bad at all. Got to have a real mind, good mind."

\* \* \*

Brian Tuesday was five when he was taken from his home at the Big Grassy River reserve on the southeast shore of the Lake of the Woods and moved to St. Margaret's Indian Residential School.

Although Brian was 18 years younger than Annie Wilson, he encountered the same oppressive conditions she had to endure during her five years at the school. Nothing had changed for the better.

The boys and girls were separated in the yard by a wire fence. Brian, whose Ojibway spirit name was Tibishkopiness, wasn't allowed to approach the fence to talk to his little sister. On more than one occasion, he stood helplessly on his side and watched as one of the nuns beat her senseless.

During the time he was at St. Margaret's, Brian was sexually abused by a priest and beaten by a nun. Things got a bit better when they transferred him to St. Joseph's Indian Residential School in Thunder Bay, Ontario—about 350 kilometres to the east, on the north shore of Lake Superior. The sexual abuse stopped. However, a big nun used to beat him with a yardstick. She broke his right forearm once when he held it up to ward off the blows.

Brian never did recover from the horrible things that he was subjected to in the Indian residential schools. His lack of self-esteem and profound sense of self-loathing was so strong that, when he was an adult, he used to smash washroom mirrors with his fist because he didn't like the look of the tortured face staring back at him.

Despite earning a Bachelor of Social Work with a major in English from the University of Toronto, Brian never adapted to life in the white world and fought a never-ending battle with alcoholism.

"I know the effects of that, what it did to me when I was sexually abused," he told me during one of our interviews. "I know what it did to me. Now I can deal with it, but the doubts, the doubts are implanted in there. Even today they [Indigenous people] have to deal with their doubts. And, as I'm speaking to you today, I know what I'm talking about. It's there. It's present. The doubts are there. We can't deal with what might have been because it's non-existent.

"If we want to achieve something, then *we* have to do it. We can't depend on the external force to come in and help us do these things. We have to do it ourselves because I truly believe that all those resources to succeed are within us if we so choose to accept them and acknowledge them, but I don't feel that we're doing that and I think it has to do with this experience in the residential school system.

"For all the damage that's been done, for all the pain and hurt that it caused, we understand all that, we know that. We do experience it. But it did something else beyond that that we don't seem to be able to grasp and, to me, that's where the blockage is. I think it's the doubts.

"We have doubts now on our bounties. We have doubts now of our own institutions. We have doubts on our own expression. So, in other words, everything that we attempt to do, I believe, reflects the Western European ideology or philosophy.

"It took me a long time to understand, to know, what was driving me to deny my own identity, to create this illusion, this illusion of being who I am **not** and expending all that time and energy to maintain that illusion. If you put that on a collective basis, you can imagine the effect it has on our individuals, on our families, on our Indian communities and on our nations."

In June, 2007, I picked Brian up at the store across the road from his small apartment in Nestor Falls, about 120 kilometres south of Kenora. As we sat at the picnic table at his favorite lookout just up the road on Highway 71, I looked down on Kagaki Lake and pictured Brian's ancestors paddling their canoes across it hundreds of years ago.

Brian was 63, and expressed pride that, despite all the demons that still haunted him, he'd stayed almost entirely sober for 18 years. He was in pretty good shape. Still living on the edge, but sober.

"I was a drunk," he told me after taking another drag on his cigarette, "I didn't care what was happening down in the next house or the condition the kids [He had three sons and a daughter.] were in. I just didn't give a damn because there was this notion that I was above all that. Even though I was abusing alcohol at the time, I still believed that I was above it all because I was educated in a white man's system and I was knowledgeable and doing a lot of things. That was the attitude.

"Drinking is one of the characteristics of a colonized person. That's just the way it is and we have to get over that. First, we have to understand that we're colonized. The way we think has been induced by the colonization process, and now we have to get back to our own [Ojibway] way of life. For a long time, in high school and all that, I denied my own people. And then, when I first went to a sweat lodge, there was a change in my head in the way I used to think, the way I conducted myself."

Brian told me what it was like to be enslaved by liquor: "You don't care about anything. You have a bottle and the next drink is all that matters. I've been through all that but I've also learned a lot from my past. Destroying your body is not the answer to a good life. Destroying your mind, your spirit. That's essentially what addiction's doing."

Brian Tuesday's life took a turn for the worse in 2008 when someone suggested he file a claim through the Independent Assessment Process—a component of the $2.8 billion Indian Residential Schools Settlement Agreement the Canadian government signed in 2006.

While preparing his submission with his lawyer, all of the horrible childhood memories of sexual and physical abuse buried deep in his consciousness bubbled up to the surface. He started drinking again. Heavily. While he was awarded $179,000 in compensation for the abuse he suffered in the residential schools, he didn't derive a nickel's worth of benefit from it.

He was still drinking heavily when he got the settlement cheque and handed the money over to his ex-wife who lived just up the road at the Sabaskong reserve. She bought herself a Buick SUV, got a new boat and built a porch around her house.

When I last saw Brian in September, 2010, he was flat broke and gaunt, surviving on fish he got from a commercial fisherman he helped out every morning. I gave him a ride to Fort Frances to visit one of his sons, who had been in and out of hospital for several years. Brian's long white-streaked hair flew in the wind as he took his son out for a spin on his wheelchair.

Over coffee on the morning before I headed back to Kenora, Brian gave me a photocopy of a handwritten poem he'd composed at a fishing camp north of Nestor Falls when he was still sober back in 1994. He also loaned me his copy of *When Rabbit Howls*, a book about a two-year-old child who created an inner world to escape the horror of violent abuse. The book clearly meant a lot to Brian.

I gave him some money and a windbreaker I'd bought for him at a local store and said I'd see him again in the spring. That never happened. Brian died alone in his small apartment at Nestor Falls less than four months later. His son told me he'd had a couple of strokes and suffered a massive brain aneurism. He was 66.

This is the poem Brian wrote when he was still sober back in 1994. He called it "The Bell."

> In the child's mind he can hear it,
> the sound of the bell.
> Like embers of a dying fire rekindled, memories stir,
> awakened, once again to revisit the madness of a time and
> place almost beyond memory.
>
> Fleeting images, glimpses of the unimaginable.
> Like a shockwave, the child remembers.
> Transfixed, he simply goes away to seek solitude in
> a world not of this place nor of this time.

Words echo.
"My child, my child, God has made a terrible mistake
Come, I must recreate you into my own image."

The child sleeps, senses on full alert. In the dorm, others
of his kind, asleep on bunk beds, row on row, pray that
tonight madness will not visit.

A slight disturbance in the midnight air—movement!
Madness is on the prowl.
Who is the chosen?
A silent scream fractures the midnight calm.
The child freezes.
For tonight madness has chosen to visit upon him
the unimaginable.
Violated in mind, body and spirit, desecrated of the
   sanctity of his life,
the child simply ceases to be.

The years have passed.
On a hilltop a man sits, bottle in hand.
Hair once jet black betrays strands of white.
Lined with age, the face mirrors a life gone astray.
He waits and waits, not knowing what it is he waits for.

Darkness approaches.
Tortured by memories which haunt his mind, he tilts
   bottle to lips,
if only to seek solace in the stupor of cheap wine.
For the man there is nothing but the emptiness and the cheap,
meaningless, high of wine-induced euphoria.
Heaven!
He succumbs to the drunken sleep
to escape the hell of a tortured mind.

It is autumn.
The season of spectral colors, with brush in hand, paints
a beautiful portrait of scenic wonders across the landscape.
Myriads of different shades and hues clothe majestic trees
in their finest attire.

The wind plays upon a flute a beautiful and haunting melody.
Mesmerizing, the beautiful music entices the imagination
to alight on wings of melody.
To journey to distant lands and times
that never were.

The child cries.

# *About the Author*

**ROBERT MACBAIN** is a Scottish-born Toronto author who has spent more than 60 years in journalism, politics and public relations.

MacBain is a former senior reporter at the *Toronto Star* and *Globe and Mail* and news director of Canada's second-largest radio station.

He is the author of the novel, *Two Lives Crossing*, and a non-fiction book on Indigenous issues, *Their Home and Native Land*.

Still living a full and active life at 86, MacBain lives in the Upper Beach area of Toronto with his wife of 40 years, former International Cooperation Minister Maria Minna.

www.ingramcontent.com/pod-product-compliance
Lightning Source LLC
Chambersburg PA
CBHW030433010526
44118CB00011B/624